FULL CIRCLE

A HANDS-ON AFFAIR WITH THE FIRST FERRARI 250 GTO

Larry Perkins & Petra Perkins

ISBN: 978-0-578-97104-9

Book design by Blue (www.bluedes.com)

For three who made all the difference:

Wolfgang (Taffy) von Trips, who innocently started it rolling with his camaraderie and enthusiasm

Wayne Obry, who closed the circle with his consummate skills and generous friendship

Scuderia di Bari, whose people understood the passions that a machine may infuse into people's lives

CONTENTS

AR TRANSPORT CORP. 42 STONE ST., NEW YORK 4, N. Y. **DUTIABLE**

BOX 87
CONSUMPTION ENTRY
BUREAU OF CUSTOMS

COLLECTOR'S COPY
ACCOUNTING COPY
STATISTICAL COPY

This Space For Census Use Only			Form approved. Budget Bureau No. 48-R217.6.	This Space For Customs Use Only ENTRY NO. AND DATE	
C AND FILE NO.	M.O.T.				
	MANIFEST NO.				

FOREIGN PORT OF LADING	U.S. PORT OF UNLADING	Dist. and Port Code 10-01	Port of Entry Name NEW YORK	Term Bond No. S.E. 5

Importer of Record (Name and Address)

LUIGI CHINETTI MOTORS INC. 750 11TH AVE. NEW YORK

For Account of (Name and Address)

SAME

Importing Vessel (Name) or Carrier FRANCE	B/L or AWB No. BACOAOCCN 6333	Port of Lading	I.T. No. and Date
Country of Exportation FRANCE		Type MARINE Invoice PROFORMA	I.T. From (Port)
U.S Port of Unlading NEW YORK	Date of Importation 7/6/62	C.O. No. PIER 88 N.R.	I.T. Carrier (Delivering)

MARKS & NUMBERS OF PACKAGES COUNTRY OF ORIGIN OF MERCHANDISE (1)	DESCRIPTION OF MERCHANDISE IN TERMS OF U.S.I.D. ANNO. NUMBER AND KIND OF PACKAGES (2)		ENTERED VALUE IN U.S. DOLLARS (3)	U.S.I.D. ANNO. REPORTING NO. (4)	TARIFF OR I.R.C. RATE (5)	DUTY AND I.R. TAX (6)	
	GROSS WEIGHT IN POUNDS (2a)	NET QUANTITY IN U.S. I.D. ANNO. UNITS (2b)				Dollars	C
CO 28793	1ST INV. PROFORMA ONE USED FERRARI AUTOMOBILE ENGINE & SERIAL # 0794 TR EXPORTED REGISTRATION #59190		INV. $5000				
	1000	1 UNIT	5000	1615.0500	FREE	FREE	
REG.141584	2ND INV PROFORMA ONE NEW FERRARI AUTOMOBILE ENGINE & SERIAL #3223 GT		INV. 7500				
	8500	1 UNIT	7500	0369.2000	7½	562.	
REG 28796	3RD INV. PROFORMA ONE USED FERRARI AUTOMOBILE ENGINE & SERIAL #3357 GT		INV. 5500				
	8500	1 UNIT	5500	0369.2500	7½	412.	
	(3)		18000			975.	
/0 ITALY							

THIS SPACE FOR CUSTOMS USE ONLY

1ST INV. FSD
2ND /3RD INV SC I

I declare that I am the ☐ nominal consignee and that the actual owner for ns purpose is as shown above, or ☐ consignee or agent of the con— I further declare that the merchandise ☐ was or ☐ was not ob—

tained in pursuance of a purchase or agreement to purchase. I also ist in my declaration all the statements in the declaration on the back of entry.

LUIGI CHINETTI MOTORS INC. 7/11/62
BY: INTRA-WAR TRANSPORT CORP. ATTY.

DATE (Signature) (Address)

☐ Principal.
☐ Member of the firm.
of the corporation. ☐
(Title)
☐ Authorized agent.

Foreword—**By Denise McCluggage**

'**ve** been around cars for a longish time. Time enough to journey through a couple of automotive eras and the marvelous transformations they've bestowed. I've driven, demonstrated, tested, written and speechified about cars and *more* cars, and some of my finest hours have been spent racing them.

Some have been very special, like my little black MG-TC and my perhaps more dramatic blue Ferrari 250 GT SWB. For my friend Larry Perkins, his red Ferrari 250 GTO has been singular too. This is a memoir of their long relationship and inspiring closure late in life.

When I met Larry, I didn't think "racing driver." He came across more as your assertive young exec with immaculate fingernails. Sporting a ready smile and his flat-top haircut, he cruised through the paddock like a small, friendly aircraft carrier. Anyway, it turned out he really could drive.

The story starts with the day Enzo Ferrari and his canny *artisti* presented a design distinctive in its time, devised from the tarmac up to win the World Sportscar Championship. It was the 1962 Ferrari 250 GT Competition berlinetta, soon and forever dubbed *Gran Turismo Omologato*. The "GTO."

No matter what it was called, the new car proved to be a beguiling, brilliant utensil to cook up trouble for competitors. Chassis number 3223 GT headed the line, and fate chose Larry as one of its lucky owners. Four years on, at Daytona, Larry was the last GTO driver to score a major class victory.

The first Ferrari GTO had claimed its own thread in the fabric of motor racing history.

After that, Larry and I ... contemporaries, competitors, friends ... had a series of long stretches between sightings. At one in 1994, Phil Hill and I were gobsmacked to discover Larry had become a sculptor—and had created a thrilling likeness of Phil in bronze.

We enjoyed a more recent encounter at the 2011 Pebble Beach *Concours d'Elégance*. There, with twenty of its siblings on Pebble's perfectly trimmed fairway, was Larry Perkins' erstwhile GTO, flawlessly restored and decked out in racing livery. And there too was Larry, who had left the Ferrari behind to take part in the race to the Moon. Until it had searched him out again.

Larry and his wife, Petra, are writers who recognize serendipity when they spot it—and who captivate us with the passions that classic cars seem to stir. Theirs is a tale that is certain to intrigue and entertain you with the way things were, racing-wise, back in the day. They are conducting a grand tour, so fasten your seatbelts for a riveting ride, complete with some twisty bits.

–Denise McCluggage, Santa Fe, NM, 2014

Denise McCluggage (1927-2015), was a noted American auto racer, writer and photographer. She was also a pioneer of equality for women in the U. S., both in motor sports and in journalism. The authors are grateful for her warm words of encouragement and inspiration during the early stages (2012-2014) of developing this memoir.

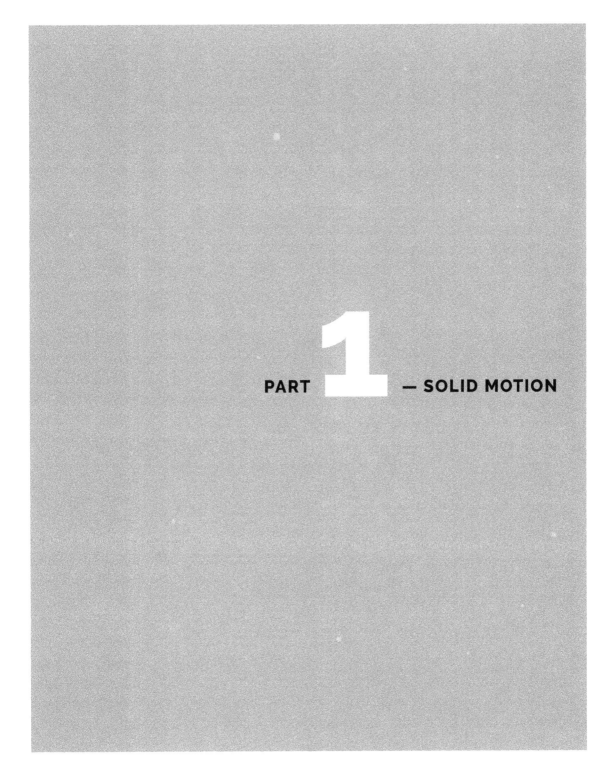

PART **1** — SOLID MOTION

Chapter 1: **Surfing at Bernard's**

t's late October 1963, just before Halloween. The corner booth in Bernard's Surf bar in Cocoa Beach near Cape Canaveral, Florida. The boys are having a couple of rounds after work. They've got their drinks—and plates stoked with happy-hour free food. The "boys" are Larry Perkins (Perk) and his cronies Jake, Pepi, Bob and Fred. They're shooting the breeze. As always, the breeze blows toward cars and racing.

The casual chatter has suddenly taken a shocking turn—not so easy with a bunch of aerospace engineers and race drivers. Larry has just made a proposal which sounds ... sort of ... like a joke. Is he playing some sort of goofy Trick-or-Treat game?

"Perk, the race is definitely going to fall to a Ferrari. If you were seriously gonna run it, a GTO's the ride you'd need. So much for your brilliant idea."

"Well, OK. But reliability's the hot tip, and they're known for it. I'm thinking even an old one—say two years?—could be made competitive. Wouldn't it be fantastic to do?"

"Who knows the Speedway better than we do? Lord knows we've turned enough laps on that thing."

"Well, for sure, but you know the factories are gonna bring the latest toys. And famous lead-foot guys like Hill and Rodriguez and Company. Anyhow, I'm pretty sure GTOs are as rare as chicken lips."

"I'll bet there's one available somewhere—for the right price."

"And what price would that be? Those damn things aren't free, Perk. Where would that kind of dough come from?"

"Hey, maybe we could take up a collection at church?"

"Nah, we can't let Jake inside a church— the place would disintegrate."

[The discourse turns silly.]

"Those little red Ferraris are so pretty ... they draw the sleekest pit bunnies."

"If we had one, what color would it be? Not red. Maybe purple? It would confuse everybody. Make 'em slow down to gawk, and we'd whip their butts."

"Yeah, or we could paint it barf green. Wouldn't hardly piss off some uppity gentleman racers, would it?!"

"Hey, wait a minute ... barf greee ... Bee Aay Arr Eff. 'Brevard Auto Racing Fraternity,' ... **BARF**! How's that for a classy team logo?"

"Pepi, you've got a new spray rig. Mal's a lettering pro. We could get him to make big stick-ons. 'BARF' on a pukey green background ... I ... can ... not ... wait."

[Raucous yucks and big swigs all around.]

"Hey, there's Fred. Come on over, Fred. We're talking a serious thing here. Perk thinks we oughta get a GTO and beat the big boys in the Daytona 13 Hours."

"A GTO? A Ferrari GTO? You guys are drunk or nuts or all three. It could never happen."

"Aw, you build fast cars yourself. You know the drill. Help us figure this out."

"When's the race?"

"February. Middle of February."

"Man, where you hidin' the opium pipe? No way there's enough time. You don't even have a car!"

"ARE there any cars? I mean, how many are there in the world? Maybe twenty? Besides, don't they keep 'em all kind of ... busy?"

"Sabiston? Maybe he knows. Could we get Sabiston to wrench on it? He's a magician."

"Yeah, John Sabiston. Perfectionist. And he knows a million tricks. I could really work with Sabiston."

"You're gonna need a quick co-driver, Perk. I mean, you're probably not the slowest guy in the world, but I have noticed it takes you a while to get over there to the bar."

[More hilarious yucks and raised glasses around the table]

"Hey, Perk, you're sideways half the time in your little bitty Cooper. What the hell would you do with a big-ass Prancing Horse?"

"Rings on his fingers 'n' bells on his toes. Round and round ol' Perky goes!"

"Aw, bullshit, guys, it's my tires. Blue Streak T3s. Hard as glass, twice as slick. Besides, my big spin at Osceola was in the rain. And Sorensen slammed the door on me."

"Ohh, yikes, tires. Where could we get enough rubber for practice and a thirteen-hour race? Maybe Robinson would make us a deal on some Goodyears?"

"Children, please repeat after me: Bill-Rob-in-son-does-not-do-deals-on-rub-ber."

"Sponsorship from Clyde the parts guy? Maybe he'd spring if we put 'NAPA' on the car. What about Charlie at the bank? He's the VP of Money, for crying out loud!"

"Maybe an airline would sponsor us … we could advertise their barf bags."

"Hey, don't laugh. Jack Slottag is getting a Porta Potty sponsorship for his Lotus."

"Uh … entry fee? What's it cost to get into one of these oversize shindigs?"

"Not too bad actually. I checked; 350 bucks. Covers garage space, fuel, pit passes, all the stuff. It's not a show stopper."

"But a pit crew could be. The tough part will be to keep a crew at Daytona during the week … it's over an hour's drive up there, and everybody's on different schedules. And getting that co-driver."

"Eve. I'm thinking Bill Eve's the guy. He's super-fast and a savvy mechanic too … gentle on the machinery. Bill's gotta be an advantage in a long-distance race."

"Tough shit, Pepi. Bill's in the Army, in Colorado or some damn place out West. He'd be out of reach. Right, Perk?"

"Not sure. I'm gonna try right away. His mom's here in town; I can probably get in touch through her."

"You serious? You're actually gonna call Bill? You sound like you're sailing your own dream boat here. Pretty sobering, man."

"Look, Jake, this is starting to be at least halfway realistic. It could be a doable do, and I think we oughta try. I've got a little money squirreled away, and it sounds like we can probably get some more. I'll start looking around for a car first thing tomorrow. And we could use some help with the grapevine too."

"OK, I know a guy. Dad's a car dealer in Cocoa, Al Hodges. He just got one of those brandy-new Pontiac GTOs for sale, and he races stock cars too. There could be a promo connection. I'll call and check it out."

"What d'ya think, Fred?"

"IT WILL NEH-VUH HAP-PEN!"

⚙   ⚙   ⚙

Bernard's Surf was a 1960s Cocoa Beach institution—if a fifteen-year-old seafood joint in a ragtag, sun-bleached, shore-side village could live up to such a lofty title.

If a person craved a beer and a mess of fried catfish after a day's work around America's emerging space port—you could visit The Pier. But if you preferred a perfectly crafted drink, upscale hors d'oeuvres and satisfying conversation, you'd stop by The Surf during Happy Hour. Hordes of Cape denizens poured through the doors. Astronauts, engineers, executive secretaries, space journalists, gawking tourists, all chattering and schmoozing, especially in the weeks leading up to a major rocket launch. The Surf at such times defined the Cape social atmosphere. It was all about going to the moon.

The Surf gained fame for a menu of absolutely fresh fish only hours out of the water— and its increasing popularity as the go-to place for visiting space race dignitaries. The shiny new Mercury astronauts gathered there. Real rocket scientists from all over became regulars. Marty Caidin, the prominent and colorful aerospace writer, was a fixture. Walter Cronkite, ex-race driver and budding TV superstar—not yet the "most trusted man in America"—often frequented a big corner booth in the dining room. And owner Bernard Fischer's hospitality was known far and wide.

Larry's racing crowd were Surf regulars, and the slightly daft decision to get The Car was reached in Bernard's bar. As for the car, it wasn't actually The Car yet. It was just a race car, but the kind you'd need to beat the factory teams in the first Daytona Continental 2000 kilometer road race. A car capable of going very fast, slowing down even faster, and enduring thirteen grueling hours at top speed on a serpentine road course and the most daunting banked track in the world.

February 1962—The car is born

Chapter 2: **The Car is Born**

Race cars are not beautiful nor ugly. They become beautiful when they win.

—ENZO FERRARI

I n the early hours of February 24, 1962, someone—someone very trusted—at the Ferrari factory in Maranello, Italy, inserts a key into the ignition of the new car they have just put the finishing touches on during the night. He gives the gas a pump or two, turns the key and listens to the starter whine ... then ... RRRHUFFAH RRRHUFFAH!... it fires explosively and the tach needle leaps to 1500 rpm. The man may sit still a minute, listening to the motor. Perhaps he's having a last drag on his Modiano, inhaling tart nicotine along with the rich aroma of fresh oil and fuel as he warms the engine, for it is late winter and gets chilly even in the exotic boot of southern Europe. The driver then weaves out the back gate, onto the Via Nazionale Abertone Inferiore, past the Hotel Planet, the Via Alfredo Dino Ferrari, through streets with empty piazzas and into a soft dawn awakening the Emilia-Romagna countryside.

As he moves through the transmission's gears on the hills, attuned to the unique song of the Testa Rossa three-liter engine, he must pass early risers such as a few farmers or bakers waving at the amazingly fast red car as it flashes by them. They could very well be saying: *"Coso diavalo é che?"* ("What the hell is that?") The man probably can't believe his luck now and must be feeling blessed to be the one testing this stunning and phenomenal machine, the world's only example, for it is the soon-to-be-iconic Ferrari 250 GTO Competition Berlinetta. This is its birthday.

Back at the factory and all tuned up, the V-12 engine is no doubt just cooling down when the international motoring press arrives, the car's trade Journalists and VIPs have been invited into the private courtyard for Enzo Ferrari's traditional press conference to unveil his latest competition cars. The presentation includes this one preening in the rising sun, a most unusual light-weight front-engined GT (Grand Touring) car capable of possibly 180 mph. Here is the swoopy low-profile of the slippery Sergio Scaglietti body style that 33 of the 36 GTOs will eventually have. Its paint is *Rosso Cina*, the classic Ferrari red, with a longitudinal Italian Tricolore stripe. The reporters and photographers gather in the lot next to the yellow Ferrari headquarters building. The car is parked at the back of the new fleet, alone, waiting to be noticed, admired, and have its birthday photos taken.

Ferrari designers and engineers peer out the windows over the crowd, probably congratulating themselves on this great achievement in high-performance race car design and sleek, low-slung beauty. One can imagine these proud Italian fathers handing out cigars for their flagship race car. But they probably aren't smoking them yet because they are holding their collective breaths.

At the time of the press conference, just two GTOs exist: this one is Serial Number 3223

A test drive through the bucolic Maranello terrain

GT, and the second, s/n 3387 GT, is behind closed doors being prepared for the Sebring 12-Hour race next month. International motor racing is regulated by the FIA (Federation Internationale de l'Automobile). FIA regulations require *at least one hundred* examples of a car to be built in order for it to be "homologated," i.e., approved for Grand Touring Car Racing. As of this day, there are only two completed cars in hand. Enzo needs to produce 98 more for homologation in 1962 competition.

The puzzled press is deflected by an official-sounding explanation—this is just an upgraded model of the existing 250 GT Short-Wheelbase Berlinetta line—a natural evolution of the design that would *not* require new certification. No big deal, right? Wrong. Under the new aerodynamic skin are a number of major design changes to improve speed, handling and reliability on the track, and it has none of the Grand Touring "creature comforts" of its predecessor, the 250 SWB. (For example, instead of beautiful hand-matched hand-stitched leather seat covers, it has plain blue cloth.) In reality, it is a thinly disguised limited-edition new *race* car.*

While this drama ensues, Enzo is dealing with staff trouble. Three months before—after a heated organizational dispute, possibly over his wife Laura's persistent interference with office politics—Enzo has fired the whole lead design team and installed a new team to pick up the ball. So, s/n 3223 GT had stepfathers who refined and completed the configuration.

The savvy press corps must be wondering when they look inside the cockpit, not seeing all the accoutrements of a Grand Touring car—such as a speedometer. There is only a center-mounted tachometer, the size of a *torta* tin, with a max of 10K on the dial. This car is not meant to be utilitarian. It is designed as a full-on highest-speed racing machine. No one yet has a clue how well it will perform, how desired it will become (except possibly the *uomo fortunato* who has just taken it out for a spin).

After its debut, the red car leaves Italy. Later, in June, it gets noticed in France at the 1962 Le Mans 24-Hour race, where it sits in the wings as a back-up race car in case one of the "real" cars fails. It may go around the track a time or two to warm up, but other than that, it's still a virgin racer. When Le Mans is over, s/n 3223 GT gets loaded onto a boat and sails for the docks of New York City. Like many other young immigrants to the U.S., its existence and future are unknown.

The first owner, Bill McKelvy of Scuderia Bear, reportedly paid American importer Luigi Chinetti about $14,000 for the car—a big sum in 1962—and raced it with a number of drivers in the Northeast and Florida through 1962 and early '63. He then sold it for about $6,000 to one of those drivers, car dealer Bob Grossman, who ran it briefly in New York and Canada. It performed as predicted, like a thoroughbred, and lived up to its initial reputation as a contender, finishing in respectably high positions in SCCA and FIA races.

Race cars don't last as long as race horses. After working like a Trojan for two years, s/n 3223 GT became a "used race car" that needed investments in reconditioning, so Grossman sold it for $10,000 (a tidy profit indeed) to a driver from Cocoa Beach, Florida, named Larry Perkins, who was searching for a GTO to fix up and mix it up at the Daytona and Sebring races.

Larry was a rather unlikely race driver because his day job was not at the track; it was at Cape Canaveral, on the Apollo space program, working with rocket scientists and astronauts to land on the moon by the end of the decade. But Enzo Ferrari had checked him out, as he did anyone who wanted to race one of his cars—for he had a consummate reputation and demanding standards to uphold—and decided that Larry, the rocket scientist and amateur driver, was good enough to race, and be possessed by, this 250 GTO.

* On its home turf, the car was never referred to as a "GTO;" the Ferrari factory's designation was "Comp/62 berlinetta" throughout its active life. The "Gran Turismo Omologato" moniker was actually a wry nickname coined by the motoring press during the homologation controversy. It stuck, and by 1964, with the Ferrari continuing to rack up victories, the tag was used so universally that John DeLorean of General Motors dubbed his impressive new muscle car the "Pontiac GTO."

Chapter 3: **A Racer is Hatched**

Racing ... because football, baseball and golf only require one ball.

~ ANONYMOUS

In his student days at Louisiana State, Larry bought a brand-new foreign car (or "*farn cawr*," as they'd say then in the Deep South). The 1959 Mercedes Benz, a pretty little thing with peerless workmanship, was an unorthodox choice. A certain echo of enmity from WWII still clung to Japanese, Italian and German products. The U. S. imported car market was sluggish, the cars were rare, and common marques were mostly British. MG and Triumph owners waved and honked to each other in solidarity.

Larry's well-to-do uncle, a "Buy American" stalwart, disowned him because of his decision, but Larry drove his flashy new ride to the nearest Sports Car Club of America meeting and joined the clan. The SCCA would be spliced into his life on and off for the next forty years.

One of Larry's first SCCA acquaintances, a fellow student named Stan, raced an Austin Healey Sprite, a diminutive English sports car that presented an odd appearance. As someone said, "Give a Brit some sheet metal, and you know he'll do something unexpected with it." With their slab-sided styling and protruding non-retractable headlights, the economical Sprites were affectionately called "Bug Eyes" or, in their British homeland, "Frog Eyes."

The Sprite four-cylinder power plants were tiny. With a 950-cc displacement, bizarre so-called "dash pot" S.U. carburetors and somewhat erratic electrical parts, they produced a Herculean 43 hp. But the little machines lived up to their impish namesake with quick, responsive performance and afforded exciting, low-budget—and limited-velocity—racing.

Stan enlisted Larry as pit crewman, changing "tyres," checking oil, refueling, keeping tabs on essentials like Stan's helmet and gloves. Eventually Larry himself was allowed to drive the Sprite one quiet Sunday afternoon on twisty lanes in a big urban park surrounding the State Capital. A mysterious disease incubated instantly; Larry became an incurable *Car Guy*. And that basic Sprite engine, known as a BMC A-block, and those quirky S.U. carbs would occupy key roles in Larry's life for the next twenty years.

As the 1959 Christmas season drew near, all the talk among SCCA folks was about the first United States Formula 1 Grand Prix. It was the last race of the F1 season, and the results would determine who was crowned World Champion. A trio vying for the honor, based on accumulated points, were Jack Brabham and Stirling Moss, each driving a Cooper-Climax T51, and Tony Brooks in a Ferrari 246.

The race was to be run at the Sebring International Raceway, a remarkable choice considering the location of the circuit (hours from anywhere), the availability of accommodations and amenities (virtually none) and the track condition (fatigued World War II airport runways and a network of lumpy service roads). The names, nationalities, cars and the contest itself were all foreign to Larry, and anyhow it was a long way from Baton Rouge, Louisiana, to Sebring, Florida. In those days of limited TV coverage, there would be no way to see the race.

But Stan had an idea. "Let's go to Sebring and watch the race live." After the usual token objections, they cooked up a plan. Pooling resources, another driver named Jim offered his tow truck, a beat-up VW van. Bob volunteered carpentry skills, Stan knew the racing ropes and Larry brought enthusiasm. Bob built a frame inside the van and layed in a pair of old mattresses ... *voila*, there was a luxurious over-under bunk. They lashed two six-foot ladders and some planks to the roof. They loaded the van with provisions and plenty of beer. And about noon on Friday, December 11, they bid their families *adieux* and pointed the VW east toward ... who knew what?

They drove straight through in shifts, eating on the run, stopping only to pee and push on, through rain, fog, blazing sun, along the Gulf Coast and down the Florida Ridge, about 800 miles—no Interstate in those days—to the obscure little town nestled in the citrus groves. Arriving at daybreak, they filched a breakfast of grapefruit fresh off the trees and, with some locals' help, searched out the track southeast of town. It was early, they gained access quickly, and with a race program they located parking on the north side of the turn known as the Esses. They had embarked from Baton Rouge eighteen hours earlier and felt they were now occupying a new section of the universe.

Larry and his buddies unloaded the ladders and planking and set up a tall mini-grandstand next to the MG Bridge a few yards from the fence, overlooking the track and above the heads of standing spectators. There were few restrictions then, and everyone around them expressed envy at this innovative spectator perch. They settled down with their beers to relax and wait.

A warm-up race for "compact sedans" preceded the Grand Prix. The boys could hear the start ... the announcer shouting a countdown on the PA, the thunder of many engines accelerating. Then the cars appeared at the Tower Turn to their left. The pack was an unlikely mix of Jaguars, Volvos, Falcons, Studebaker Larks, Saabs, a Hillman, Corvairs, Renaults and a VW, scrambling and crowding through the turn and down the short straight, pounding under the bridge and through the Esses, rounding the Big Bend, disappearing down the straight toward the Hairpin, their clamor fading from earshot.

Then ... silence.

Well, not quite. With a muffled snarl, a tiny white Fiat 600 sedan came into view, driven by a large man with a proper helmet but dressed in a blue blazer with brass buttons, a white dress shirt and a red necktie. He wrestled the car through the Esses, seeming to fight for grip ... or theatrics ... and slowly followed the others out of sight. Everyone looked around and joined in a huge incredulous laugh. Who *was* that clown?

When the cars came through again, widely strung out and led by a Lark, there was a much longer delay before the Fiat appeared for a repeat performance. But that was the last they saw of the driver in the sport coat and tie; he must have been black-flagged. The race continued and was eventually won by a Jaguar, to no one's particular surprise. The crowd was warmed up, and the Formula 1 big boys were staged for the main event.

An hour later, the *Star-Spangled Banner* filled the air, followed by a colossal roar from the grid as the green flag fell on 18 Grand Prix cars and a hopped-up dirt-track midget racer being bravely hustled along by top USAC driver Roger Ward.

As the race cars made their first trip at speed through the Esses, it was obvious to Larry that these were a different breed of animal. The cars carried their national racing colors— Italian red, British racing green, German silver and, a concession to the American driver on home turf, a blue and white Ferrari for Phil Hill. Even as a newcomer, Larry found that this multihued parade looked, sounded and acted quicker. Something about their stance as they went through the corners was so much more in tune with the track, and they were obviously very much faster than the sedans ... or the USAC midget. Someone explained that the cars were all custom-built by factory specialists and were equipped with sophisticated power plants, adjustable suspensions and innovative disc brakes. They howled as they streaked by; something about them *smelled* different. And they ran *so* close together with those open wheels!

The '59 USGP was won that afternoon by New Zealander Bruce McLaren driving a factory Cooper. He finished 0.6 seconds ahead of Frenchman Maurice Trintignant in another privateer-entered Cooper. Briton Tony Brooks was third in a Ferrari Dino 246. Australian Jack Brabham ran out of gas on the final straight of the last lap and finished

Jack, Bruce and Larry at the Esses

fourth. But he led the season's championship points total and so was awarded the first of his three world titles, as well as the first such for an Australian, for the Cooper factory and for a rear-engine car. Four driver nationalities, two manufacturing countries and a revolutionary new race car design were all on show in the first four places. The rough Sebring circuit had taken its toll: American Phil Hill DNF'd with a bad clutch after only eight laps, and the great Stirling Moss retired with a blown gearbox after just five laps. But finishing sixth in a Ferrari was a young German named Wolfgang von Trips.

As the excitement wound down, Larry and the boys dismantled their private grandstand and stowed it on the van roof, shared a final cooling round of beer, and headed for Baton Rouge. They were home bright and early on Sunday morning, having more information about the famous race than the morning sports pages. Hardly anyone could believe they had made that trip. Larry could hardly believe what he had seen and heard ... and felt there.

After the amazing Sebring adventure, studded with so many multinational influences and technical exotica, Larry was well into the clutches of racing fandom. All that darting and jousting in close quarters by the world's best drivers had riveted him. The brightly painted cars in motion were like fine art. Aromas of fuel and Castrol and burnt rubber and hot metal and brake dust were like drugs. He heard music in the engines' roar and a thudding scuff of tires under stress in corners. He wondered, "What would it be like to actually do that myself?"

The following year, he continued to support Stan's racing efforts, occasionally pit crewing through the spring and summer, but all his other time and energy were devoted to finishing school. He graduated with honors from the LSU School of Geology, Class of 1960 ... and couldn't find a job in the then-slumping oil industry.

He signed on instead with Colgate Palmolive, moved to St. Petersburg, Florida, and became that butt of rude jokes—a "traveling salesman." He covered the Florida west coast, from Crystal River to Everglades City, hawking household soaps and cleansers to grocery accounts and supermarkets. It was not exactly the path to mineral riches he had anticipated.

But owing to a mild climate, Florida and the Southeast supported very active year-round motor racing, and Larry soon fell in with the SCCA's Central Florida Region crowd. He became acquainted with the road racing community and was befriended by Gordon

Pennington, who owned and raced the very first Ferrari 250 GT Short Wheelbase berlinetta (s/n 1539 GT.) He found the look, feel and sound of that burgundy-hued, bellowing V12 bombshell mesmerizing. And his new friend Gordon turned out, astonishingly, to be the stealthy Fiat driver in dress clothes whom he had watched with such amusement at Sebring the previous December.

Larry was thus exposed to "real" racing action, accompanying Gordon and his wife, Margi, to Nassau Speed Week and the Sebring 12 Hours of Endurance, where international professionals and awesome machinery waged aggressive head-to-head competition.

The participants, whose names were still unfamiliar to Larry, hailed from all over the world map and motor racing spectrum: Stirling Moss, Dan Gurney, Jo Bonnier, the Rodriguez brothers, Denise McCluggage, Jim Hall, Roy Salvadori, Roger Penske, Hap Sharp, Phil Hill, Brian Naylor, Gaston Andrey and many others. The paddocks were an egalitarian hodgepodge of drivers, car owners, team mangers, nobility, sycophants, crews, journalists, celebrities, groupies, beauty queens, free-loaders and well-dressed guests.

Larry met Ferrari owner/driver Bob Grossman, who would later figure in his personal story, and a Nassau Speed Week fixture, Red Crise. Red was a flamboyant promoter whose energy, wits and somewhat irascible style had created the event and kept it going year after year. Most everyone enjoyed Bahamian island pastimes, such as sailing and snorkeling, and attended gala social events at the home of Lady Greta Oakes, owner of the racetrack and a competitive Austin Healey driver in her own right.

At Nassau's Oakes Field, a leading German driver named Wolfgang "Taffy" von Trips treated Larry to some heart-stopping practice laps around the racecourse in 1539 GT's passenger seat. Safety rules were, in a word, very relaxed.

"Grab a helmet, Larry, and we'll take a few turns round the circuit."

Von Trips was a winning driver on the Scuderia Ferrari Grand Prix team and was soon to be vying for the 1961 Formula 1 World Championship. His skill behind the wheel left Larry in a daze. The speed was electrifying. The car's agility made it all seem ... well ... effortless.

Taffy had a genteel, easy-going manner and total fluency in English (as well as Italian, French and, of course, German). Over drinks he and Larry engaged in long discussions of braking, cornering, overtaking, handling traffic, racing philosophy and, most of all, smooth technique. Larry was unaware of Trips' nickname in European racing circles: "Count von Crash."

Larry's first ride with Wolfgang Taffy von Trips

Sebring, compared to Nassau, had a different vibe. The social atmosphere gave way to more intense competition, and the stakes were higher on the international calendar. The twelve-hour race and the primitive track put phenomenal demands on people and inflicted merciless pounding on machinery. Everyone was a bit more focused and winning was a big accomplishment for any team. The DNF rate was high, and just to finish Sebring was, and still is, a feather in anyone's cap.

Teams spent much of a week at Sebring, though, and there were opportunities to relax. The remote hamlet in the citrus groves seemed vaguely isolated from reality. The old Harder Hall Hotel, with its attractive golf course, adequate dining room and high ceilings, lent an air of tired elegance and timeless leisure. Pretty lakes studded the area. Orange blossoms had begun to spread their charming perfume. Only occasionally did anyone come upon an alligator.

It was all extremely intoxicating for the junior soap peddler.

After his exposure with Taffy von Trips and the others at Nassau and Sebring, Larry became convinced that he needed ... must have ... a proper car to go racing with. His

Mercedes was definitely not it. Despite that sedan race at Sebring, domestic cars were mostly used in oval track competition, and a few like the Chevy Corvette were seen in road racing, but the lion's share were imported marques—MG, Triumph, Sunbeam, Austin Healy, Porsche, Ferrari, Alfa Romeo, Lotus and, at the bottom of the list, Fiat.

⊕   ⊕   ⊕

Larry's commuter ride to work was a Fiat 600. It was not awe-inspiring: a pug-nosed, two-door sedan, even shorter than a Sprite, with a smaller, rear-mounted engine pumping out a prodigious 29 hp. But to Larry it had all the best attributes of a race car—four wheels, brakes, a motor, and he owned it.

The fearsome Fiat acquired a roll bar and a fuller-throated exhaust system and shed its chrome hub caps. In quick succession, Larry attended the necessary meetings, driver schools and club races and earned his license with the H Production "pygmy racer." Getting around a road course, even with a little Fiat, still required all the driving basics if one was to avoid embarrassment. And Larry's bedtime reading became the all-time

Fire-breathing race car - Fiat 600 D

A real Cooper BMC giant-killer

champion book of driving, Piero Taruffi's *The Technique of Motor Racing,* which he consumed, cover-to-cover, multiple times. He would drop off, and wake in the morning, reciting the cornering mantra: *Lift, Brake, Shift, Turn, Gas.*

At last, Larry worked his way into a National License, running against Sprites, MGAs, Spitfires, Minis, Berkeleys, Karmann Ghias, ring-a-ding Saab Sonnets and petite Fiat 850 Abarths (oh, what cars!). He didn't win any races, but he learned how to smoothly get around a circuit in a reasonable hurry and stay out of trouble while doing it.

Hankering for a *real* car, Larry moved up to a Cooper Formula Junior—a whole new ballgame. An open-wheeled single-seater, with a Cooper factory-built, twin-carb BMC-A engine amidships, it boasted 100 hp in a 900-pound car. With driver aboard, that was a ratio of about 10.5 lbs/hp (vs. 49 lbs/hp in the Fiat). Cam response was abrupt but steady, up to a 6,800 rpm redline. The drum brakes were integrated into alloy wheel rims for weight and heat reduction. Rear tires were wider; weight distribution was near 50/50; the oversize radiator and oil cooler assured no engine overheating. The body shape was torpedo like, and driver seating was low in the chassis, maybe eight inches off the pavement.

The cockpit was Spartan: four gauges displaying the vitals and one dash-switch to start the engine. It was a snug fit for a guy Larry's size, with foam padding taped here and there to reduce driver bruising when banging through corners and traffic around the circuit.

There was little knee room, and the pedals were set far forward and close together. A welded-up aluminum fuel tank was mounted in the nose above the driver's legs.

There was no generator or alternator in back, so the starter was used sparingly, allowing the tiny garden tractor battery to last through a race weekend without a recharge.

Visibility from the driver's seat was completely unobstructed. The windscreen was just a deflector, set below the driver's eye level, and side-mounted mirrors were aimed to spot cars sneaking up from behind on either side. The exposed front wheels were right under the driver's nose, as it were, so one could sight along them, precisely following the correct line.

Larry's Cooper office

The Cooper was a tight, efficient little package and an enormous pleasure to drive fast. The sting of grit, water, pebbles, oil, small car parts, toads and rubber fragments blasted against one's face by cars in front didn't diminish the fun one bit.

In that era, SCCA starting grids often contained mixed classes, including fendered and open-wheel cars with a range of performance. Thus, Larry's competition could typically include Fomula Jr, the new Formula V and Formula S plus an assortment of C, D and E Production sports cars (Porsches, Triumphs, Healeys and the like). The Cooper was quick and nimble, capable of winning races against larger classes, and Larry began doing that. A crop of engraved silver cups, trays, bowls and statuettes began growing on a shelf in his garage.

In the U.S. Southeast of the 1960s, a person who was willing to tow a few hundred miles could literally race nearly every weekend. National, Divisional and Regional events were held in venues from Atlanta to Savannah to Central Florida and the Miami area. The circuits varied from rough repurposed airports to baby-butt-smooth new tracks. But facilities tended to be minimal, and often far from urban centers, so competitors needed to be highly self-sufficient. Parts availability was particularly scarce. Larry's club racing morphed from a hobby into a serious, demanding, expensive, long-distance, time-consuming obsession.

And all this time Larry had an itch, set off in 1959 and stoked at Nassau in 1960, to run with the "big boys." He was still a working stiff in the aerospace industry, but he ultimately became possibly motor racing's least likely privateer. Thus began a five-decade journey that would come full circle.

Chapter 4: A Good Car is Hard to Find

Never think of your car as a cold-blooded machine, but as a hot-blooded horse.

—JUAN MANUEL FANGIO, 5-TIME WORLD CHAMPION

The 1963-64 winter season was an eventful time in America. President Kennedy was murdered in Dallas the week before Thanksgiving. In his honor, on New Year's Day New York's Idlewild Airport was renamed John F. Kennedy International and was promptly walloped by a massive blizzard. At the end of January, NASA's Saturn SA-5 put a nineteen-ton payload in orbit, proving to Americans that the Apollo Program was making progress in the race to the moon. A week later the Beatles landed and started driving a whole nation of teenage girls out of their minds.

And a week after that, an event occurred that completely consumed Larry Perkins' attention—the first Daytona Continental 2000 Kilometer endurance race for sports cars. Everyone in racing knew in advance that this thirteen-hour international event would be won by an already iconic Ferrari 250 GTO. Thirty-three GTOs existed, and some number of them would compete at Daytona. The only question was, which one—with what driver— would take the prestigious trophy?

Larry was determined that it would be him at the wheel of his own car. Discussion with his cronies at Bernard's Surf had concluded that he could do it when it snowed in Hell. But with persistence and luck, he had located two GTOs, both in the USA. One, with a high asking price, was s/n 4219 GT belonging to Bev Spencer in California. The other, a well-used one with a friendlier cost, was s/n 3223 GT owned by Bob Grossman in West Nyack, New York.

Grossman was asking $12,000 "negotiable," and he didn't make entirely clear what shape the car was in. Larry arranged to meet with Bob after New Year's, and assuming all went well, they would consummate the sale of one of the only GTOs to be had anywhere. Larry was unaware that s/n 3223 GT was The Very First 250 GTO. He probably wouldn't have given a damn.

One night in early January, Larry caught a red-eye to JFK, grabbed a Hertz rental, and drove up the river to West Nyack. Arriving at Grossman's VW dealership around 6:00 a.m. he scrunched under his thin Florida trench-coat and snoozed in the car for a couple of hours. It was cold, but in those days weather forecasting was largely done by reading tea leaves; there was no hint of a looming snowstorm. When Bob arrived for the meeting, he came upon Larry's sleeping form and no doubt surmised he had some sort of nut on his hands. The price could have become non-negotiable right then and there.

Initial discussions opened over coffee and donuts at a local diner while the guys got re-acquainted—and compared racing experiences—and Bob learned of Larry's modest intent to beat the world in the historic Florida race (which Bob also planned to run with a new Ferrari). Then it was time to go back to the car store and have a look at the GTO. Except there was no GTO at the store.

See … Larry had already been in touch with John Sabiston, a master racing mechanic who ran the Pit Stop Garage in Bayshore, New York. He had been referred by Larry's friend, John Bentley, who with Jack Gordon had won the 1960 Sebring Index of Performance. Sabiston had wrenched on their victorious OSCA 750. Sabiston, a forceful, self-confident type, had been to West Nyack and run Grossman's Ferrari a little. Although its condition left something to be desired (including "blowing a little blue smoke"), John had convinced Bob to let him have the car, which he had driven, racing livery and all, down the Palisades, across the George Washington Bridge, through the Bronx and Queens, over highways and byways to his shop on Long Island! Well, it was a GT car after all.

So, with the car unseen, some bargaining went on, and Bob came to realize that Larry seriously intended to run the race less than two months hence, and he had Larry squarely over a barrel. A deal was struck for $10,000 (equivalent to about $85,000 in 2021 dollars), which was an attention-getting introduction to big-time racing. Larry had no title, Bob had his check but no cash in hand and John already had the drive train out of the GTO before

Larry's first glimpse of his future

Larry could say, "Ooops-I'm-Not-Exactly-Sure-I-Really-Wanta-Do-This!"

All that was left in Grossman's garage was a stack of Borrani wire wheels, a little box of parts and a couple of oily spots on the floor. Larry loaded the rental car with these spares—no mean feat as the car was small, there were at least eight wheels and some still had worn tires mounted. Then he shook hands and set out for Sabiston's place. It was noon on the first day of this absurd life-altering escapade.

Larry had never seen a GTO. He would never forget this first glimpse of *his* GTO in a gloomy corner of the Pit Stop Garage. The car was up at a crazy angle on jack stands, was streaked with grime and seemed to have been gutted. The motor hung forlornly from a cherry-picker over the engine bay, and the rest of the drive train lay scattered on the floor. The iconic GTO shift lever stuck straight up like a flower stem from a bouquet of bolts, nuts, washers, strap hangers, shafts, gaskets and hand tools. But the machine had a certain sleek feminine aura. After all, she *was* a Ferrari, she *did* have a bright red-and-white livery and she had big black race numbers ..."**30**"... on proper white roundels. But she definitely did not yet look like a world beater.

After arranging with John for the next day's activity, Larry contacted friends on Long Island's north shore, who invited him over the following evening. He found a decent motel and good seafood on the waterfront. He was fed, watered and could bunk in for a well-deserved night's rest. As improbable as it seemed, he was the owner of a world-class race car, and the pieces were falling into place to run a world-class motor race. Though he was burning a candle at both ends and the middle, Larry probably should have considered the weather an omen. It might have been "snowing in Hell."

Larry woke the next morning at 6:00 a.m. with snow falling. At the Pit Stop he and John went over preparation of the car, which had recently run shorter events with little maintenance but hadn't run an endurance race since the previous Sebring. There was *plenty* of work— and logistics. How to get the car to Florida during winter along the eastern seaboard? Was minimal paperwork in order? Should they just run Daytona or follow with Sebring, 150 miles away, a month later? What parts were needed from Luigi Chinetti's Manhattan shop? What about budget? As plans were being thrashed out, mechanics were furiously dismantling the GTO. In less than *six weeks*, the green flag would drop on a 2,000-kilometer race.

It had been snowing all day as Larry prepared to visit his friends in Smithtown. The Hertz rental had no snow tires, but the scrap pile behind the Pit Stop yielded lots of heavy stuff, so the guys let a bit of air out of the tires and filled the trunk with junk. The car squatted like a toad, but it moved nicely in the fresh snow. Larry set out across Long Island into the teeth of the worst blizzard to hit New York in years.

Later that night, after Larry said his goodbyes, he found his car nearly buried, the battery unresponsive. (1960s batteries were less resilient than today.) He hitched a ride to the city jail with a policeman and spent the night sheltering in an open cell with a troop of coughing, snorting, spitting, farting, barfing, mostly drunk vagrants.

The bums grumbled, bitched and made dumb "no maid service" jokes. No one on Earth knew where Larry was. He desperately needed to finish up and get home to Florida, but he knew the planes weren't flying. He was a snowed-in, cut-off, budding entrepreneur; to this day he can recall the aroma of that jail cell.

Kicked out at six the next morning Larry approached a snowplow driver for help. His battery was duly jumped and Larry took off, wallowing along on half-flat tires with his trunk-load of junk. He called the airport from his motel. (Pay phones were where you found them; cell phones didn't yet exist.) They had re-opened and a single flight to Orlando was departing at three. He packed, zoomed over to the Pit Stop, made last-minute arrangements, and tore out of town toward Idlewild … now JFK.

Besides nearly running out of gas, getting jammed in two snowbanks and having his hood latch fail, letting the wind wrap the hood over the windshield, his trip to the airport was uneventful. The poor car galumphed along, clattering and wailing, but got him there. It was 2:00 p.m. as Larry rolled into the Hertz garage and took off running. He arrived as the gate was closing and was forced to plead almost in tears for an exception: would they please, PLEASE let him on the plane?!

At last, the flight lifted off for sunny Florida. A couple of days later, Hertz called, trying to figure out what had happened to their nice little Ford over the weekend. It had been dropped off with:

- No paperwork
- No keys
- Two flat tires
- Its hood nearly ripped off and secured with a coat-hanger
- Its driver's door nearly ripped off and secured with an expensive silk necktie
- Its trunk full of car parts weighing 180 pounds
- Its trunk lid secured with mechanic's wire
- Its interior soiled with mud, snow, ice, debris and bits of tire rubber
- An empty gas tank

Larry later wrote on the incident report that the car had been buried in a drift and must have been hit by a snowplow. It was known to happen.

At Bernard's Surf in Cocoa Beach, the gang gathered to hear the story. Larry bragged a little and said that when Sabiston finished his magic, the car and the race would be everything they hoped for. All crowded around to catch every tidbit about the amazing, already legendary Ferrari GTO.

Larry didn't even have a picture of it.

⊕   ⊕   ⊕

Preparation of s/n 3223 GT for that first race was rocky. One must imagine the difficulties with getting parts, trick fluids like Shell 250-weight differential grease (who ever heard of 250-weight lube?), various unwritten specs and obscure Ferrari tricks unknown to Sabiston who was a genius but had never before rebuilt a Ferrari V12.

Larry, in Florida, had his full-time day job. His "new" car was 1,200 miles away, and his only tool was the telephone. The whole deal turned on a common principle in racing back then ... "I give you my word."

The rest of January and February were frantic. The car was in pieces on Long Island and everything had to go together and get down to Florida. John made repeated trips to NYC for parts from Luigi Chinetti's Ferrari HQ. Larry phoned the wide world over, finally finding, in England, a 9:32 "Le Mans" rear-end ratio for the Daytona Super Speedway circuit. Air freight costs mounted. The newly rebuilt engine was started for the first time **one hour** before the car was driven onto the trailer.

It was a major berzerka. Pit crew to organize. Accommodations to arrange. Goodyear tires to order. Larry's co-driver, Bill Eve, had to get Army leave in Colorado and fly to Florida. Time was closing in. Daytona practice started on February 12, and the race was on February 16. Money gushed out in a relentless green torrent.

Help for the latter came from Cocoa auto dealer Al Hodges. In return for using the race car in a promotion for its namesake, the new Pontiac GTO, Al provided space in his stock car shop, use of a dyno, money and general support.

Cocoa, Florida; Saturday, February 8:

It was done. On time. They had managed to get the mostly ready car from New York to Florida, not entirely without incident.

At around 3:00 a.m. on an inky, frigid February night, somewhere south of Richmond, John was towing the GTO on an open trailer (the way everyone, including the top teams, did it in those days) when he nearly lost it. His monster black Cadillac, doing maybe 100 mph, came onto a bridge coated with black ice. The whole rig, nearly 40 feet long, lurched sideways and, without touching the railings, skidded to the other end, wheels spinning and aimed in all the wrong directions. With a miraculous save—part braking, part see-sawing the wheel, part divine intervention—John (an old dragster driver) got it sorted out, put his foot down and kept on trucking. His passenger, Warren, reported it this way, "I didn't see a damn thing. I had a death grip on my rosary and my eyes squeezed shut!"

When Larry heard the story later in Cocoa, he thought, "Hey, maybe I should have THIS guy for my co-driver!"

Race Day was one week away. The BARF team had to be in Daytona on Wednesday evening, in time for early practice on Thursday. They did the "GTO twins" promo on Sunday—a Pontiac GTO alongside the Ferrari. The Al Hodges showroom was alive with bright balloons, banners, Muzak, wide-eyed shoppers and salivating salesmen. To everyone's surprise and pleasure, the dealership took orders for three of the pricey new muscle cars. Then the crew worked Monday and Tuesday on final prep, checking lists and packing for the trip up the coast.

At that point, the car had been run only enough to drive it onto the trailer in New York and off again in Florida. The brakes were brand new. The engine—double-overhead cam V12 with six dual Weber carburetors and dual ignition—was freshly rebuilt. New valves, springs, gaskets, electricals, clutch, everything. It was destined to be zooming around the track in a couple of days, and the piston rings hadn't even been seated.

Solution: break it in by driving to Daytona on public roads. It was, again, a Grand Touring car. They planned to take it on a seventy-five-mile grand tour. Bill Eve had worked his magic with the U. S. Army and was now on hand. But neither he nor Larry had yet sat in the seat or pushed the pedals, so this would also be a chance for them to learn the car. They felt a certain amount of urgency.

The sleek red form glittered in the Florida sunshine ... low "anteater" snout at the nose, high and chopped off at the tail; Goodyear Blue Streaks on gleaming wire wheels; ivory longitudinal stripe; and snow-white roundels on sides, front and rear, sporting the big business-like **32;** and front fenders emblazoned with a prominent Al Hodges logo. The car had lights, token mufflers, windshield wipers and a Florida dealer plate secured beneath the tail spoiler ... but no bumpers.

The journey began. With an edgy deep-throated snarl, this marginally street-legal ride, this super-fast jewel from Maranello, whipped out of the family sedan dealer's lot and on to a lightly used back road, *en route* to the Daytona International Raceway and destiny.

A little caravan formed, two of the crew following in a car with a CB radio, scouting in all directions for troopers. The rest brought up the rear in a heavily loaded pickup, towing the empty trailer. Being stopped for running a race car on the public highway would do severe damage to their schedule—not to mention putting a big dent in the treasury.

The drill went like this: Bill and Larry would each drive half the distance to Daytona. John rode scrunched into the passenger space, knees to chest* watching instruments and shouting directions: "**punch it**;" "coast in gear;" "let 'er suck oil;" "**punch it**;" "run flat for a while;" "**repeat**" ... hundreds of times, all in second and third gear out of a possible five. The process was an old race mechanic's trick for seating the rings and valves, breaking in the rebuilt motor in a hurry.

The noise and heat inside the cabin were nearly intolerable. The Ferrari GTO looks from the outside like a swoopy two-seater sports car, which is what "berlinetta" means. But it is in fact a race car, and a super-lightweight one at that. So, it is not blessed with interior sound or temperature-suppressing insulation—or real cockpit ventilation below 100 mph. Rather, it's an aerodynamic aluminum wrapper for an ear-splitting 300 hp oven!

The old two-lane asphalt from Cocoa to Daytona has been long-since scraped from memory by construction of the I-95 superhighway. But back then it was a gorgeous scenic route, passing through marshlands studded with palmetto thickets and pineywoods, crawling with wildlife.

The GTO rolled through the woodland, the big V12 making its trademark shriek, shattering the serenity and doubtless perplexing alligators and otters, orchids and oxeyes, hares and herons with a high-pitched blast they would hear just this once and never again in their lives.

Thus did BARF duly arrive at the Speedway with a smooth-running, more familiar plaything. There were tips along the way of stunning potential, which they would soon unleash on a proper track. Despite the GTO's outwardly forgiving ways, it was still a road rocket, and of course they were rocketeers.

As restored in 2011, s/n 3223 GT has a proper passenger seat and footwell, allowing one to sit naturally and stretch one's legs. In 1964, however, there was a kind of fixed test panel under the dash that blocked the footwell on the right side. The seat, mounted on hinges over a large battery, tipped steeply forward, so a passenger could only crouch sideways in the confined space. John Sabiston, on the way to Daytona that day, rode for over an hour bravely hunched into a cramped ball like a roly-poly.

Early Loves (and Significant Others)

It is not surprising that the GTO was passionately revered before entering Larry Perkins' life. First were the Scuderia Ferrari designers who built and tested the 250 GTO in 1961.

- **Giotto Bizzarrini**: initial designer of the GTO 250 focusing on aerodynamics
- **Sergio Scaglietti**: designer overseen by **Mauro Forghieri**—collaborated on body design
- **"Wild Willy" Mairesse**: first test driver of s/n 3223 GT's development prototype on the track at Modena and on public roads at Maranello
- **Luigi Chinetti Motors Inc.**—Jun/62 brought s/n 3223 GT to the United States from Italy
- **Bill McKelvy, Scuderia Bear**—Jul/62 first owner, purchased for $18,500. Painted blue with a white stripe. Over the next year Scuderia Bear became a consistent winning team in races with the following drivers:

First Race

- **Ed Hugus / Charlie Hayes**: Sep/62 Bridgehampton

- **Lorenzo Bandini**: Dec/62 Nassau

- **Charlie Hayes / Lorenzo Bandini**: Dec/62 Nassau

- **Charlie Hayes**: Dec/62 Nassau

- **Glenn "Fireball" Roberts / John Cannon**: Feb/63 two races at Daytona

- **Charlie Hayes / Dough Thiem**—Mar/63 12 Hrs Sebring

- **Charlie Hayes / Gene Hobbs / Alan Patterson**: Jul/63 Marlboro 6 Hrs

- **Charlie Hayes / Bob Grossman**: Sep/63 Bridgehampton

- **Bob Grossman**—purchased the car in Sep/63 for $5,500; drove it in Canadian GP Sep/63 Mosport, winning 14th Overall. (After March was repainted red with white stripe.)

The car was always run in America and Canada, with a successful racing record, winning some first or second places in category and often finishing high overall. But by the time Larry got the GTO, a lot of work was needed—and as they used to say in the Old West, "It had been rode hard and put away wet." In December 1963, Larry rode to the rescue.

Chapter 5: **Riding an Italian Stallion**

Daytona Beach, Florida - Thursday, February 13, 1964

Imagine yourself standing in a vast three-sided cement-and-asphalt bowl sprawled across the landscape, baking in the Florida sun. Its giant maw waits to swallow the unwary, chew them up and spit them out against its unyielding barriers. Welcome to the Daytona International Speedway.

It's not like any other place on Earth. Racing people call it "the Speedway" or just "Daytona." Two and a half miles around, it boasts a 3,000-foot-long back straight and two steeply banked turns inclined at thirty-one degrees. Retaining walls circle the rim to keep wayward race cars from soaring off into the Daytona Beach Airport next door.

Since its opening to much fanfare five years ago, no one has yet discovered how fast you can actually go on this swiftest of all tracks. Its creator and NASCAR founder, Bill France, is offering $10,000 to the first car/driver to average over 200 mph for three laps.

[The feat was finally achieved in 1987 by Bill Elliott's Ford Thunderbird at 210+ mph.]

THE RACE

This weekend will inaugurate the Daytona Continental 2000 Kilometer. At 1,230 miles, it will be twice the length of the classic races at the Nürburgring, Spa Francorchamps, and Monza and roughly half the distance of that daddy of them all, the 24 Hours of Le Mans. Running on a special road-racing layout, Bill France has arranged for "his" event to last thirteen hours, one longer than the famed 12 Hour Grand Prix of Endurance held every March at Sebring, Florida less than 150 miles away.

Pundits expect that the Daytona winner will likely come from the ranks of Ferrari 250 GTOs that have ruled the global Grand Touring category for some time. Or perhaps it will

SPEED

be one of the newly threatening Shelby American Cobras. Out of fifty-four entrants, eleven GTOs and ten Cobras are listed. (Note: At the moment only 33 GTOs exist anywhere in the world; a third of them are entered in this race.)

THE TEST

One of the drivers, Larry Perkins, is preparing to go pretty fast here himself—taking his first laps with the new car around this formidable track. His crew is keyed up too; his chief mechanic, John Sabiston, scarcely hides his apprehension. His quicker co-driver, Bill Eve, is hoping for the best. All are anxious to see whether Larry can handle a serious thoroughbred race car in big-time professional competition.

Cars haven't always been in Larry's blood. He's owned a few unremarkable ones, and his current commuter ride is a tiny Fiat. But he recently made a turn in the road. He joined the Sports Car Club of America, attending driver school and immersing himself in the sport. Last year he bought a glistening red Cooper Formula Jr, now crouched on its trailer in the garage at home. For him the formula car was a new kind of critter—an open-wheeled single-seater meant to be driven at the limit all the time. It really seemed less a "car" than a piece of sporting gear for his new hobby—motor racing.

Picking the fine line

But the hobby has quickly morphed into an avocation. He has become a hard-driving competitor and shown substantial skills at the wheel. He has earned an advanced license and adopted a credo popular in those circles: *Racing is life; everything else is just waiting.*

He has bought an example of Enzo Ferrari's noblest rolling stock, the 250 GTO, a Gran Turismo Omologato, and a moment of truth is bearing down. He has not driven his GTO at speed—and only heard its engine run yesterday morning. And *this* morning he is taking it out for practice on the Speedway.

Larry has thrust himself into a whole new reality. Of the four dozen men slated to drive the top-rated cars, including World Champion Phil Hill, Larry has by far the least experience. He has been active in a lower, amateur category for just over a year.

He's aware of the speculation going around. Folks who know his background seem to think he's on some sort of kamikaze mission. No wonder there's some eye-rolling in the pits. Their expressions say, "Perk, what are you thinking?"

His little Cooper has a one-liter, 100 hp engine and weighs about 900 pounds. Today he'll tackle the big three-liter GT car—at 300 hp and 2,100 pounds, a thirty percent increase in power-to-weight ratio. But Larry's tongue-in-cheek attitude is: "My day job is 'rocket scientist,' so I might as well try out my very own rocket!"

THE CAR

The Ferrari 250 GTO is rated in the Grand Touring class, a hybrid between a deluxe sports car and a serious racing machine. But the GTO's design leans heavily toward the latter. It's fitted with the minimum in legal road equipment—lights, turn signals, wipers, horn, mufflers—but no creature comforts. There is no carpeting, no glove box, no ashtray, no sound or heat insulation, not much venting. No interior door handles or roll-down windows. No cup holder.

But the GTO includes the maximum in endurance racing features—a high-revving three-liter dry-sump six-carburetor V12 engine, massive disk brakes, a five-speed gearbox, plenty of lightened components, and hand-formed aerodynamic aluminum bodywork. It sports a huge radiator and oil cooler, but no power-robbing fan or other accessories. Fuel consumption is about 8 mpg, so a thirty-four-gallon fuel tank in the rear is good for just under three hours or so on track at speed.

There's no roll-over bar or cage; the thin aluminum roof is supported by a lightweight hoop. The dashboard is minimal, dominated by a king-sized tachometer centered among

Promoted to a bigger office

the gauges. The top end of the tach scale reads "100," indicating 10,000 rpm.

Unlike a road car, there are oil temperature and fuel pressure gauges and no speedometer. It's all designed to win long-distance endurance races at speeds well above 150 mph for many hours or even days on end. The Ferrari 250 GTO is definitely a big boy's toy.

10:00 A.M.

- The track is open for practice. Cars circle, some with engines buzzing, some thundering, some—especially the Ferraris—shrieking along the straights. People often liken the sound of an accelerating Ferrari V12 to ripping a sheet of canvas: vvvvrrrrreeeeeeEEEEEEEEPPpah!

- Drivers dive into Turn 1 next to the pits, slowing and downshifting—brruppuh, ... brruppuh—then get hard on the gas, entering the short road course that winds around the lake in the Speedway's infield.

- Five turns, then back onto the tri-oval for the flat-out run to the Start/Finish line and Turn 1 again.

- The drivers circulate, lap after lap, learning the track, getting up to speed, checking tire wear, testing and tuning the cars, testing and tuning their own performance.

At last it's time for Larry to discover which way the track goes, where the tricky parts are and how the GTO, and he himself, will take to it.

The pit crew has run the engine, getting everything nice and warm—oil, water, electrics—and checked tires, brakes, all the settings (including the tell-tale). The car sits in the pit box, seeming to wait impatiently for something exciting to happen.

Like the other drivers, he's suited up: blue cotton coveralls, freshly "fireproofed" last night with dips in boric acid and 20 Mule Team Borax; no long-john underwear though— this is Florida! (Nomex fire suits are still a couple of years in the future.) String-back leather-palmed gloves; Bell Shorty open-face helmet; cotton crew socks and leather loafers (secured with duct tape to prevent slipping off). No ear plugs (he's spurning the only thing available: nasty little clumps of wax-impregnated lamb's wool ... *yuck* ... but his hearing will pay dearly in years to come). No goggles required; this is a closed car. He chuckles to himself, *It's really a luxury ride*.

Larry has a bit of a contortionist's moment, tucking himself into the seat ... the roof line is just forty-seven inches from the ground, with a high door sill and the steering wheel set at a low angle. But once he's in place it's a snug, comfortable fit with the controls—wheel,

At speed on the Daytona high banking

gear-shift, pedals, dash switches—"all ready to hand" as the British say.

Visibility is good, with a wide windscreen, big rear window and adequate views to the sides. But there are two aspects peculiar to this car: (1) the front fenders rise on right and left, in two seductively rounded swells, potentially blocking the driver's view of nearby roadside obstacles and (2) there is only one mirror, a conventional interior unit mounted on a stalk above the windscreen.

It will later develop that this mirror is nearly useless on the Daytona high banks and under heavy braking elsewhere. When the road rises up behind, or the car's nose goes down in front, one can see nothing in the mirror but asphalt or sky. No amount of adjusting will fix this. There's a strong temptation to mount outside mirrors, but the crew hasn't done it (and notably, neither has any other GTO team). Since the rear view is limited, Larry wonders, *"Do you suppose Enzo assumed no one would ever overtake his GTOs?"*

Describing Larry's first ride requires a quick overview of the road-racing course. It's 3.81 miles long, combining nearly all of the NASCAR tri-oval with a twisty infield section. A level back straight, more than half a mile long, connects the west and east banked turns. The direction of travel is counter-clockwise, typical in American-style oval-track racing and retained here.

There are ten turns in all, the first five traversing the infield, flat as a pancake. Turns 6 and 7 comprise the 31-degree west banking, and Turns 8 and 9 define the identically constructed east banking. Turn 10 is part of the front straight, not in fact straight but also curved and banked at 18 degrees.

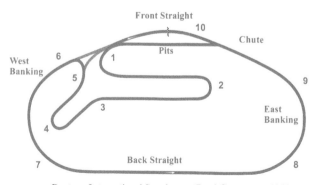

Daytona International Speedway -- Road Course - ca. 1964

The front straight passes between the pits and main grandstand, with the Start/Finish line at its center. Approaching it from Turn 9 is a relatively short, flat "chute," with a conspicuous bump where the infield entrance tunnel passes under the track. The front straight ends at Turn 1.

To give an idea of how steep the

Daytona high banking is, a car must go about 100 mph to avoid losing traction and slipping steadily down to the bottom. It's even tricky for a person in rubber-soled shoes to walk up or down it. (For sailors, consider that a heeling sailboat will tip about twenty-five degrees. A motorcycle rider in a turn leans his bike a bit more than that.) So, a thirty-one-degree bank is dramatic and, since it is also curved, it restricts front and rear visibility. The driver feels like he's in a big barrel, pulling Gs, pressed against the surface. The track ahead disappears upward at the top of the windscreen and behind in the rear-view mirror. A good way to check what's ahead is to glance through the left *side* window!

OK, it's time for Larry to get the show on the road.

He snaps the bulky seatbelt latch, *clack*, turns the key and listens for the fuel pump's electric *tick-tick-tick*. He gets a whiff of fresh gasoline and watches for the pressure to come up. He gives the accelerator a couple of pumps, pushes the key in to run the starter and fire the engine—*ruh, ruh, ruh ... brrrrufffah*. He lets it idle a bit to get its juices flowing, blips the gas a couple of times to clear its twelve throats—*brrrRUFFFah, brrr-RUFFFah*—checks the gauges again and decides all look good—GIRI "**1200**," BENZINA **4/4**," "BENZINA **4** kg/cm², "ACQUA **90°** C," "OLIO **5** kg/cm², "OLIO **80°** C." He grips the thin wooden steering wheel, fingers the smooth alloy shift knob on its oddly tall stalk. It all feels right.

Strolling on the Speedway

Larry presses the clutch in and shoves the shift lever into first gear. He waves to his anxious pit crew, flicks the turn signal to pull out, gets a "go" signal from the pit steward, raises the revs to 2000 rpm, eases the clutch out, feels the tires grab with a chirp and—kills the engine. *Shit.*

Red-faced, avoiding the incredulous glares of his crew, he goes through the motions again, catches a few more revs and this time—*vvrrrrrooooom*—at last, **at last**, Larry is on his way.

Many cars are circulating now. The pit lane merges into the left side of Turn 1; protocol dictates that entering drivers stay left, gain speed briskly and merge into traffic. The track is wide and up ahead is Turn 2, a 40-mph right-hand horseshoe, with room to run two- or maybe even three-wide. But Larry has never been here before, nor driven the car over 30 mph, so he is damn busy in this first stretch.

He arrives at the turn in third gear at around 3,500 rpm, drops to second and checks the mirror, searching for the racing line, alert for the yardage markers so he can begin memorizing the track. He rounds the turn on the outside edge, almost in the dirt, giving way to two other guys overtaking on the inside, who leave him in their dust as all head down the short straight to Turn 3. Whew, he's made it!

Larry can tell he needs to use more revs, but he has just left the pits and already the GTO amazes him. He has never experienced this kind of acceleration steadily up through the gears without faltering. He will later recognize that the V12 Testa Rossa engine is one of the world's all-time great racing tools. Once "on the cam," at around 4000 rpm, it never runs out of *oomph*. If a driver gets careless, he can rev it right past the red line in any gear until this supremely capable machine finally gives up and disintegrates.

Inside the cockpit, Larry notes the muffled engine wail—plus a clamor created by the whine of the drivetrain, air rushing over and through the bodywork, fluids gurgling, cold brakes squealing at every corner, the suspension thumping, stressed tires chirping, and vibrations large and small all over the place.

SPEED

On with the first lap: Turn 2 exits onto a short straight just long enough for Larry to accelerate and upshift once. The next corner is a quick dog-leg to the left, taken nearly flat out, promptly followed by a sharp right-hand switch-back. The good line for this sequence is to stay far to the right down the straight, upshifting to third gear, touch the brakes and turn in, moving sharply to the left edge (caution; there's no curb) to make a quick squirt through Turn 3. Then lift, brake and downshift to second for Turn 4. Clear the apex late, move to the right and be on the gas, rolling briskly in third at Turn 5. This will carry speed up onto the west banking (Turns 6 and 7) and begin the long run down the back straight. That stretch will be taken in fourth, upshifting to fifth at 7,500 rpm or more, and is by far the fastest part of the course.

So now for the quick part. A little more explanation is probably helpful:

To attain good lap times at Daytona, it's vital to set up the car for maximum speed on the long stretch from Turn 5 to Turn 1, even allowing some performance concessions in the infield. Good visibility and constant driver attention are essential because in endurance racing cars from many classes, with different performance levels, compete together. The speed differential between the slowest and fastest cars on the back straight may easily approach 100 mph.

For example, a Ferrari GTO approaching an MG from 100 yards back, the length of a football field, might only take two seconds or so to overtake and pass. It's vital that drivers anticipate such events. The contrast becomes even more critical as dusk turns into night. (Note: in 1964 there was no track lighting beyond the front straight and pit area.)

Heeere we go! Larry thinks. At first, dropping off the west bank and accelerating down the back straight, he hesitates to put his foot down. (Soon, after a couple of shake-down laps, he'll sense that his times aren't up to snuff and he'll get more determined.) Now he goes up through the gears, shifting at 7,000 rpm, and settling on 6,800 in fifth. The GTO is in its element, eating ground, and wailing like a banshee.

Along with the commotion, it's hot. Any race car is a bit of an oven. That lovely V12 motor, as well as the brakes, running gear, the track itself, all blast heat through the un-insulated aluminum firewall, floor and drive-shaft cover—straight into the driver's space. A five-gallon tank behind the passenger seat collects 200-degree oil from the engine. The windows are closed to maintain aerodynamic efficiency, and the "passenger cooling vents" are a joke. This all raises the cabin temperature to around 140° F (60° C) on a warm Florida day. The driver's footwell gets even hotter, and one wears rubber-soled shoes at his peril—feet will go numb in half an hour. The GTO cockpit is a true symphony of noise, heat, and visual and inertial stimuli, with nothing to dampen or diminish any of it.

Everything may look smooth as gravy to an outside observer, but all hell is breaking loose in the driver's seat. The whole car complains as the din from engine, gearbox, drivetrain, tires, bodywork, road surface, wind becomes literally deafening. The hood and front fenders flutter as if they'll depart any second; doors rattle; windshield wipers start an unstable jitter, creeping up the glass. The steering gets featherlight, and the car feels like it's dancing on the road. Larry has already given up any illusion that this is a luxury ride!

Straight ahead, the east banking seems to grow higher. Closing at this speed, Larry's peripheral vision narrows, and that sweeping turn towers like a vertical wall ahead. At 160 mph, "driving on ice," this is definitely a time for rapt attention.

An obvious thought dawns on Larry—this car is *not* a rocket, and it is *not* flying. It's rolling on four rubber tires, hurtling down the Daytona back straight with him as the "pilot more-or-less in command." It's anchored to Planet Earth by just four contact-patches totaling about 320 square inches … the area of an open coffee-table book.

And poised less than a foot above said Planet Earth is his butt.

Aiming into any corner, a driver's backside detects the car's attitude change first. One gets a tiny directional tug in the seat of the pants. Then the G's build until one feels some real side-force. If the car tends to "push"—understeer—the front end will try to go straight ahead. If it oversteers, the rear end will jerk around in a spin. The butt's job is to let one know in time to make corrections. Drivers who don't pay attention to their butts end up getting them into all sorts of trouble.

Heads up, Larry! Fast cars overtaking on the right … a GTO and a Cobra … V12 delivering the *soprano* high note … *vrrreeEEEEeeeeeeeee* … V8 thundering the *basso profundo*

Don't try this at home

… *bbrrumMMMMmmmmmmm* … and they're gone, ahead, down the straight. *Jeez*, he thinks, *how come they're going so much quicker than me?* But there's no time to ponder … the banking is HERE … RIGHT NOW!

Larry aims for the middle lane, lifting his foot a bit, backing off to maybe 6500 rpm, turning left just a tad, getting that little butt tug—and around he goes, tipped like a banking airplane, body pressing firmly into the seat, elbows tugged down by G-force, drumming over the asphalt cracks and patches—and there are plenty of them.

He notes the black crisscrosses on the road ... there are plenty of those, too ... the tire signatures traced by spinning cars, twisting up, up, to the right, until they stop ... WHAM! ... at multi-hued scrape marks on the unforgiving wall at the top.

Larry licks his lips, a bit sweaty and salty, and braces his left shoe firmly against the little footrest. He's not ready just yet to run close to that forbidding wall. He follows a mid-line and heads downhill into the chute. He stays on the gas, bringing the revs back up. Mustn't lose momentum in the stretch before the Start/Finish line.

He's keeping to the right now, along a less daunting straight wall. *Alley Oop!* ... a near-weightless hiccup over the hump. *Whoosh* ... past the north-side gate, where a random breeze can give the car a surprise lane-change to the south. Past the "Y" at the pit lane entrance. Staying high and close ... big letters ... D A Y T O N A ... flashing by ... so close ... crossing the Start/Finish stripe ... time to shut off for Turn 1... NOW.

WRAPPING IT UP

Lifting, Larry aims for the outside line; gets haaarrrddd on the brakes—dropping into the decreasing radius turn—*oops, watch for that slow Porsche on the inside*! Double-clutching for the downshifts ... *d'dunhh, d'dunhh, d'dunhh* ... now in second, touching the apex, he gets back on the gas, up to third, *vvvrrrrreeeEEEpah*, drifting a bit to the right, heading for Turn 2.

Wow! ... our hero has completed his first "OK" lap of the Daytona Speedway with his beautiful, howling, ground-shaking Ferrari GTO.

His lap time = 2 mins. 38 secs. An 87-mph average; not terrible but definitely not wonderful. Lots of work to do. But he has about 500 more laps to turn this week ... each, he is sure, better than the last. This coming Sunday, between 10 a.m. and 11 p.m., he and Bill will ride this hot Italian stallion, in daylight and dark, as fast as they can go for 1,200 miles or so.

By coincidence, the same day down in Miami, a British band of teenage musicians called The Beatles (Beatles?!) will turn pop culture on its head forever. But Larry and the rest of the Speedway denizens are unaware of it; they're totally preoccupied with ... **The Race!**

Postscript— random notes from the Speedway experience:

FASTER FASTER!

In some ways, a race car and its crew are just a life-support system for its engine. Preserving the power plant is absolutely crucial—mechanically, competitively and financially. So, imagine their surprise when Larry's team learns, before the race, that during practice they've been setting the rev limit much lower than is typical for their engine. "No wonder those other guys are going so much faster than us!" Hooray! There's more speed to be had at over 1,000 rpm higher, without fear of hurting that amazing Ferrari V12!

John, the chief mechanic, will instruct the drivers on what redline he wants for the conditions in the race. He relies on them to maintain that limit, but in "trust but verify" mode, he'll relentlessly monitor compliance with an indispensable gadget: the tell-tale.

TELL-TALE

- Often called a "spy," the tell-tale is a friction-mounted needle on the tachometer dial. As the white rev counter needle advances, it pushes the bright red spy with it, but the spy stays at the highest rpm (revolutions per minute) the engine has turned. It's the chief mechanic's engine- protection gizmo that shows whether the driver has over-revved even once during a run. The reset knob is strategically located in an obscure spot behind the dash, so an embarrassed driver can't nix it before coming into the pits.

REFUELING

Children, how often must I tell you? Do not play with gasoline!
Few particulars at the Daytona Speedway were more riveting than the refueling regulations. With roots deep in NASCAR's "moonshiner" legacy, they mandated the use of so-called "dump cans." Overhead gravity-fed refueling rigs with hoses and shut-off nozzles were specifically banned. Competitors in the 2,000 kilometers event were required to follow the dump can rules.

The custom-built cans, with 11-gallon capacity, extended pour spouts and vent tubes, could dump fuel into a car tank in eight or ten seconds, *if* they were handled by super-fit, practiced crew members. The cans weighed about seventy pounds full, and three were needed to refuel a GTO during a frenzied pit stop.

BARF never recorded the amount of gas spilled on the car and the ground, but over the course of the week, the asphalt pit box pavement became so softened they had to lay

No smoking allowed

plywood panels to support the snap-jack wheels. The crew offered up a prayer of thanks that they didn't have a devastating fire, but the Shelby Cobra team didn't have such good luck. During a stop for the Dave MacDonald/Bob Holbert Daytona Coupe, a fuel spill ignited, and a raging fire ensued. No one was injured, but the #14 car was instantly disabled on the spot.

(This rough-and-ready refueling method, vastly improved, is used by NASCAR to this day.)

TINY LUND'S LESSON:

On that first day of practice, "Tiny" Lund, a very big NASCAR driver in every sense of the word, strolls through Larry's pit and looks the team over. Tiny, himself entered to race a mighty Cobra, is intrigued with the low-profile, delicate-looking, wire-wheeled Ferrari. He bends way down, studies the car inside and out (especially noting the absence of a roll-cage), raises an eyebrow and drawls skeptically, "Ah y'all goin' up on th' bankin' in THAT?!" When they affirm that's the plan, Tiny decides to share some of the tricks gained from his many miles of oval track experience and help these newcomers stay out of trouble.

Tiny's principal lesson is to stay high, as close to the outside wall as possible for the given conditions. To quote him, "Y'all don't ever wanna hit that wall goin' straight ahead ... it'll hurt a lot. So don't run down low 'less'n ya hafta." He goes on, "It takes some gittin' use' to, 'speshly in traffic, but someday it'll save yer ass." *

Larry gets a sharp reminder of Tiny's advice during practice that very day. A rival driver leads Larry's down the chute toward Turn 1, both running near the wall. As the first driver applies the brakes, a glittering shower of sparks bursts around him and he spins, backward ... WHUMP ... into the wall, hard, but at a fairly shallow angle.

The car bounces off the wall and rolls down into the infield near Turn 5. Larry worries about fire, so he continues around and slows coming through Turn 4. He spots the driver standing in the infield grass, leaning on the car's roof, his form sagging, his face ashen. A wire wheel collapsed and sent him into the wall; the windshield has popped out, and the car looks seriously bent. But there's no fire and the driver seems OK. They exchange thumbs-up and Larry carries on. The low-impact angle has just saved that guy's ass.

NO SURPRISE—THE TEAM IS EVERYTHING

Hardly anybody has a greater tolerance for self-imposed discomfort than a race driver. His or her chosen work entails sustained pandemonium and stress. Larry would never be able to do his job without his team's total support. They encourage him, teach him tricks, gently scold his mistakes, and have faith in him to listen, learn and execute. The team includes Bill Eve, one of the most accomplished co-drivers in the entire field. And through hundreds of hours of hard work, their crew has furnished Larry and Bill with one of the all-time great breeds of Italian prancing horses—the incomparable Ferrari 250 GTO.

1964 DAYTONA CONTINENTAL 2000 KILOMETER RACE RESULTS:

As the gurus predicted, Ferrari 250 GT cars placed 1st, 2nd, 3rd, 5th, 9th, 11th and 12th. Larry's team, in their first international endurance competition, ran 1,126 miles and placed 11th Overall, racing against—and beating—some of the great drivers and teams of the era. They were all pretty proud of that accomplishment.

* DeWayne "Tiny" Lund died in a big crash at Talladega in 1975. He did not hit the wall. In 2001, the great Dale Earnhardt did hit the Daytona wall at a steep angle. Running low and fast, he unexpectedly turned up, across traffic and struck head on. He died instantly of a basilar skull fracture. His crash gave impetus to universal adoption, in all forms of motor sports, of the HANS device and other life-saving head restraints.

The GTO's heart and soul

Tiny Bubbles

To a driver, a race isn't so much distance, or elapsed time or so many laps. It's a long series of tense little cornering episodes. Race position must be protected; drivers must display mastery. The race's essence is in the turns, and there may be as many as 6,000 of them in a long contest.

Every corner is a tiny time bubble, maybe five seconds long, with its own space and no past or future. A lot happens—nearly all at once. It's a snapshot of perfect execution. The tiniest screw-up means losing irretrievable time. Or worse, altogether losing the corner—spinning off, waiting, helpless, watching everyone else thunder by in a humiliating parade.

When arriving at a corner, going say 150 mph, the driver replays a precise little script in his head:

"Pick up the marker... lift (now) ... brake (hard)... shift (down) ... turn in ... touch the apex...on the gas (hard) ... we're outta here!"

Seven simple steps...ever consistent...always subtly different.

Clearing the corner, pedal-to-the-metal, the driver exits the bubble and puts it out of his mind. On the straight, there's a moment to adjust the line, check the gauges, fix one's makeup. And survey the road ahead for landmarks. At this level of concentration, the driver adopts tunnel vision. Those guys you see waving at the pretty girls trackside? They're not racing ... they're teasing.

Another shut-off marker looms alongside, and a new bubble begins. At racing speeds, markers are crucial. Depth perception isn't sufficient, isn't precise enough for this high-speed, on-the-spot work.

PART **2** — BLAZING TRAILS

Chapter 6: **Moon Racing**

Well, Larry, after you've landed an armed jet fighter on a carrier at night, with no lights, in a pitching sea, driving a race car is a piece of cake.

—CHARLES "PETE" CONRAD, THIRD MAN ON THE MOON

People race. People race on bicycles, airplanes, sailboats, skis, skates, bobsleds and horses. They race dogs and bullfrogs and each other on foot. Ever since the first two cars were built, people have raced them too. Nations race, driven by an ever-present compulsion to dominate, to prove to all others … and themselves … that they are winners. That they are the best of the best.

There's something about racing … something primordial about the human need to compete head-to-head. Maybe it's rooted in the fundamental business of getting enough to eat. If you didn't get to the prey animal first, you would probably miss dinner—and maybe have to sleep alone in your cave.

From time unknown, our ancestors have been awed by the Great Bright Ball in the sky.

Sometimes it seemed ever so distant and sometimes just a stone's throw away. They yearned to reach it, but no matter how far they trudged across the land, they never seemed to get close enough. Going there had long been mankind's new frontier.

"New Frontier" was the slogan of the recently elected Kennedy Administration. And so, beginning in 1961, the world's two leading nations—the

USA and the Soviet Union—were locked in an all-out effort to set foot first on the moon. In fact, it was a Space Race.

Larry felt luckier than most people to be working at Cape Canaveral when the race began. Larry's day job was devoted to the nation's Apollo Lunar Exploration project, with its ostensibly scientific objectives. He enjoyed a ring-side seat and direct involvement in that historic contest with the USSR—while also running a two-car team, eleven months of the year, here on Earth.

But racing is a deep commitment. Some would call it an addiction. To the extent the latter might be true, Larry was fully addicted. He kept a daunting personal schedule; working on the space race; maintaining a family life and attending car races on the side. In fact, all that competition was like having two or three hard-to-please families. Larry developed a sincere appreciation for what one can accomplish by transforming each day into a thirty-two-hour endurance event.

The Moon Mission: The Apollo Lunar Landing program began in earnest in 1961 when U.S. President John F. Kennedy, in an address to Congress, proposed a national goal of landing a man on the Moon and returning him safely to the Earth by the end of the 1960s—nine short years. Kennedy later emphasized in a speech at Rice University that "we do these things not because they are easy but because they are hard. Man, in his quest for knowledge, is determined and will not be deterred." Kennedy might have channeled our audacious ancestors by mentioning George Leigh Mallory, famed mountaineer. Mallory, when asked by a reporter in 1923 why he was so intent on climbing Mount Everest, the highest peak on Earth, replied, "Because it's there."

At the risk of understatement: The trip from Earth to the Moon—and back—is immensely hard. The obstacles are staggering and the achievement so extraordinary as to defy belief. In fact, many people across the globe still don't accept that it was ever done. But, despite lots of urban folklore to the contrary, it was. How do we know? Because Larry, among thousands of others, helped bring it about.

For people employed in the aerospace industry—especially those who worked at Cape Canaveral—space, like Everest, "was there" too. So, this new national thrust was massively exciting but sobering in its test of our abilities. At the time of JFK's speech, the Mercury Program had successfully flown just four missions, two in low Earth orbit, for a total of slightly under 10.5 hours of manned space flight, each with a single astronaut aboard. Not an auspicious first lap.

By that same time, the Soviet Union had already opened up a lead. They had orbited Yuri Gagarin in 1961 and had flown the Vostok 3/4 dual-manned mission for sixty-four orbits and nearly four days in space. The race to the moon was truly on.

Reaching the finish line was roughly defined by this strategy:

- Launch a manned payload on a trans-lunar trajectory
- Coast for three days in interplanetary space
- Orbit the moon
- Land men on the surface
- Conduct EVA (extra-vehicular activity) and collect surface samples
- Launch crew on return trajectory (three-day cruise)
- Touch down for an ocean rendezvous
- End the mission with a recovery ship

In the fall of 1962, almost none of the crucial items to support the mission existed yet: • Launch vehicle and support facilities • Apollo spacecraft and lunar landing module • Flight control centers • Computers and software • Manned spaceflight criteria • Flight readiness test procedures • Thousands of trained staff

The people: In all of mankind's history no endeavor of this complexity, precision or magnitude had ever been attempted. A tiny number of people had any exposure to aerospace work; a huge new labor force would be built on the fly: engineers, technicians, testers, astronauts, software developers, trainers, human resource experts, financial planners and managers. Aside from administrative positions, there were very few women.

Much of the work was unique and had no precedent. Many otherwise qualified people didn't know at first how to do their jobs; they adopted trial-and-error methods and perfected them as the project went on. (This also described the situation facing Larry's racing team in their first endurance event!) But America steadily learned how to be a space-faring leader.

Not least in the leadership role were America's astronauts. Early on, thirty were selected based on flying experience and rigorous testing. Several of these, test and combat pilots with a special taste for speed, engaged in spare-time boat and car racing. They kept a low profile to avoid NASA's wrath. An accident that took out one of these highly trained people in a mere hobby would be an inexcusable loss. But, by nature, they were gluttons for competition.

By the mid-60s, Larry had become an SCCA drivers school instructor. Several astronauts attended the school during assignments at the Cape: Pete Conrad and Al Worden for driver training; Rusty Schweickart and Gordon Cooper for support (anticipating his upcoming lunar mission duties, Rusty was never without a Hasselblad camera in hand). Jim Rathmann (recent Indy 500 winner) along with his wife, Kay, an accomplished driver in her own right, who supplied the guys with Formula Vees to attend the school.

While Larry had introduced many novices to the task—art?—of racing, he had not seen drivers with such aptitude as Conrad and Worden. They were quick and precise right out of the box. As they patiently pointed out, they were physically near perfect and had spent many hours flying the best jet fighters our country had to offer. Going fast was part of their DNA.

THE PROCESS, OR "HOW TO GO TO THE MOON IN 7,650,000 EASY STEPS"

Any Apollo overview seems to describe a fantasy project, so formidable and unforgiving as to seem unattainable. But Werner von Braun, titular father of our space program, advised, "I've learned to use the word *impossible* with the greatest caution." Larry added, regarding both the work and his team's racing ambitions, "No one accepted that it couldn't be done—so we pushed hard on the 'go' pedal and did it anyhow."

And it was fun. For example, as a Saturn V stage contractor, IBM built the Instrument Unit (IU) stage, which housed the vehicle's "brains"—computers controlling the rocket from liftoff through flight into orbit. During long countdowns and tests, the unit was complex for operators to maintain error-free control. Larry was an IBM systems engineer assigned to develop solutions. So, over several months, he and his colleagues created a computer-driven "Launch Countdown and Checkout Training Simulator," with the unpronounceable acronym LCCTS. Their nickname for it was "Count Checkula." The project was so challenging, and so successful, that Larry said he would have gladly worked on it for free.

Larry's racing team members also worked at the Cape during the Apollo era. They found some basic principles that applied equally to running a space project or an endurance racing effort:

- People are life-support systems for brains; treat both as precious commodities.
- Humans are fragile; design—and test—for their survival.
- Requirements are key; define needs, not nice-to-haves.
- Deadlines are demanding but utterly necessary.

- Reliability and risk reduction count; leave nothing to chance.

- Test 'til you drop.

- Everything takes longer than you expect, and "Murphy's Law" is real; if something can go wrong, it probably will.

- Follow the Scout motto: *Be Prepared*.

- And never ... ever ... be late for meetings.

All was not smooth sailing on Apollo. There were failures due to human errors, design problems and even a certain amount of overconfidence.

In 1965 two giant Crawler Transporters were built to convey the 9 million-pound Saturn Vs and their mobile launchers from the Vertical Assembly Building (VAB) to the pad. They were the largest self-powered tracked vehicles in the world, and during initial testing, they blew their traction bearings. Going back to the drawing board for a year, the builder ultimately reduced the units' rated speed from 3 mph to 1 mph (which it remains to this day). Not exactly race cars.

The most dramatic and tragic setback occurred on January 27, 1967. During a normal launch rehearsal test, a flash fire swept through the Apollo capsule and astronauts Gus Grissom, Ed White and Roger Chaffee perished. It would take extensive spacecraft redesign and exhaustive testing and retraining for more than eighteen months before a reliable capsule was back online. It was also necessary for NASA to overcome public resistance to continuing the program.

The Money: It was understood from the outset that a manned lunar mission would cost a bundle. But as Kennedy had insisted, the space budget was "somewhat less than we pay for cigarettes and cigars every year." The Apollo Program would ultimately cost the country about $25 billion ($158 billion in today's dollars), which in reality was quite sustainable. Through it all, the project sped on.

By comparison, managing the Brevard Auto Racing Fraternity's tiny budget was taxing for its principal, Larry. All the bills got paid, though no final accounting of costs to race the GTO has been preserved. But it was surreal for the little privateer team to work by day on that big NASA money gusher and balance their meager checkbook by night.

Larry's crew, despite daunting schedules, technical issues and fatigue, sped on. At 11:00 p.m. on February 16, 1964, their Ferrari 250 GTO finished their first long-distance race, the Daytona 13-Hour Continental, placing 11th Overall in a highly competitive international field. They were over the moon!

And on July 16, 1969, a Saturn V super-booster thundered into the Florida sky, riding a 1,000-foot tail of flame, hurling its precious cargo into a colossal unknown. Neil Armstrong, Buzz Aldrin and Mike Collins would have a flight unlike anything they—or anyone else—had ever experienced. After three days' cruise through outer space, their spellbinding words came crackling over the radio: *"Houston; Tranquility Base here. The Eagle has landed."*

Five days later the Apollo 11 crew capsule plummeted through its fiery reentry plume and drifted sedately on its three candy-striped parachutes, down to the Pacific Ocean. JFK's promise of landing men on the Moon and returning them safely to the Earth had been met with phenomenal success.

The U.S. had taken the checkered flag in the Moon race.

The USSR had suffered a DNF.

The ultimate checkered flag

Science In Racing

During Thursday afternoon practice, a couple of nice young guys visited the BARF team pit and introduced themselves. They were physiologists from the University of Florida at Gainesville, and they were studying effects of heat and fatigue on athletic performance. They had invented a compound that should be superior to water in preventing dehydration and exhaustion. They asked whether the drivers would be willing to participate in a lab experiment.

Larry Perkins and Bill Eve did not think of themselves as athletes, exactly, but they had to admit they experienced plenty of heat and fatigue on the racetrack. The team also had little interest in distractions but, being the new kids on the block, they decided they could benefit from some added attention among the more entrenched teams. They agreed to a low-impact effort to support the scientists.

The procedure: Record driver's vitals—temperature, blood pressure, heart rate, urine samples. Have the drivers drink a half-liter or so of the "secret elixir"... a pale cloudy liquid that tasted like a mixture of toilet cleaner and weak lemonade. Then, have them go out and drive their brains out for a couple of hours.

At the next pit stop, the scientists would close in to take vitals again, and make meticulous notes about the drivers' perceived comfort level, alertness and energy reserves. The bottom line, according to Larry was, "I don't know what the hell this stuff is, and I hope it doesn't poison me, but it works, and I feel great!"

What it was ... was *GATORADE*. Named after the Florida Gators football team, it was eventually packaged, flavored, and commercialized as the very first sports drink. Gatorade has been successfully marketed ever since. It's an electrolyte-laced solution designed to control fluid balance in the brain and tissues of a person undergoing performance demands. It reduces thirst and fluid loss through sweating and enhances endurance and a feeling of freshness.

But whether it's orange or red, yellow or blue, or flavored like fruit, Larry remembers it as a flask of lab chemicals, and to this day he does not allow a drop of it pass his lips.

Chapter 7: **The Crucial Crew**

Your mom called, Larry. She says it's time for you to be home in bed.

—JAKE JACOBSON, PIT CREW

I t's often said that "the car's the star," and the driver's the leading member of the supporting cast. But racing is an intensely collaborative effort, with the driver as a component, and the entire cast is essential. The combined energy of the team, particularly in endurance racing, paves the path to success. Winning without it is nearly impossible.

Larry's team adopted a whimsical name, BARF (Brevard Auto Racing Fraternity), taken from the area they called home: Brevard County, Florida. It seemed less pretentious than, say, "Scuderia Superiore" *(Super Troupe)* or "Maghi dallo Spazio" *(Space Wizards)* and the indelicate double-entendre appealed to the group's irreverent attitude.

The following are brief profiles of BARF's mostly volunteer crew members, who brought dedication, unique skills, rugged staying power and plenty of off-beat humor to the game. Some of these players worked together on a series of racing projects for over six years, and the four surviving members maintain contact to the present time, 2021.

Note: Although the following group seems large, they were seldom together at one time, except at the track for a long race. Different people were present for different events, and

all had day jobs and were scattered geographically, in Florida and New York. Just managing their whereabouts and schedules was a challenge in itself.

John Sabiston: chief mechanic. Day job: garage owner, Bay Shore, New York. John had many years of experience as a driver, car-builder and expert mechanic in drag racing, stock cars and long-distance sports car competition. His manner could be imperious, and he was absolutely uncompromising in terms of precision and thoroughness. When he took over preparation of the V12-engined GTO for the first time, he had never touched a Ferrari before. But when John said it was OK to go, it meant everything was done—correctly—and you went. Sabiston saved BARF's bacon many times over.

Bill Eve: co-driver. Day job: U.S. Army PFC. Bill brought an established reputation from his years of racing in SCCA and an initial foray into the professional USRRC series. Bill was recognized as a meticulous mechanic and a very quick driver with a light touch in every car he tried—skills that were highly prized in any endurance effort. Bill demonstrated his prowess at the first race by keeping pace with World Champion Phil Hill in a like car, prompting Hill to take notice of the BARF team. An extra benefit was that Bill and John Sabiston "clicked."

Ken "Jeff" Jeffers: crew chief. Day job: propulsion engineer, Titan III Launch Vehicle. Jeff was a deeply immersed car guy enthused by all forms of racing ... midgets, sprint cars, Indy, F1, stocks, dragsters, sports cars, anything with four wheels and a motor. His mechanic's skills rivaled Sabiston's, and his crew management approach was firm, thoughtful and strategic. Larry traveled with and drove for Jeff for several seasons, learning something valuable at every race and enjoying every trip as Jeff was hugely entertaining. But Larry was always an obedient driver as Jeff was six-feet-four and could adopt a withering demonstration of disapproval.

John "Jake" Jacobson: crew member. Day job: aerospace technician, Apollo Lunar Module. Jake drove an Austin Healy and an Elva in SCCA and contributed a thorough all-round knowledge of racing requirements. Jake had an unquenchable, zany sense of humor that helped lighten up difficult situations, but he was an acute, observant crewman who could be serious when necessary. Jake contracted amyotrophic lateral sclerosis in the late 1960s, which unfortunately shortened his life in midstride.

Jake with pit board; Pepi on the right

Raymond "Pepi" Kelso: crew member. Day job: auto mechanic. Pepi was a seasoned mechanic, spending years in various forms of auto racing. He knew what was needed and he knew how to do it. Pepi could also be demanding and did not suffer fools gladly, but he clicked with Sabiston and was a definite asset. Like most BARF members, he had a quirky sense of humor. Pepi was never without a cigarette hanging from his lip, and a favorite trick, when strangers were around, was to quench the burning butt in a random pool of gasoline. After scaring the daylights out of them, Pepi would patiently explain that "it's only the *fumes* that are dangerous." Larry was never convinced Pepi was entirely right about this.

Bob Rodamer: crew member. Day job: aerospace engineer, Titan III Launch Vehicle. Bob was an experienced SCCA driver, with the fund of racing lore that implies. He thus had all the needed skills for a crucial crew member, plus he was a steadying influence on more excitable characters—like Larry, for example. Bob's cool, deliberate manner made him a highly dependable, smoothly coordinated member of the team.

John Brooks: mechanic. Day job: garage owner, Fort Myers, Florida. John was the mechanic for Jack Slottag's Lotus 23B and Russell Beazell's TVR Grantura. He was

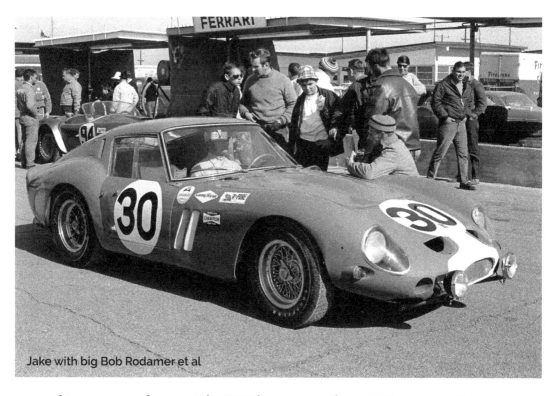

Jake with big Bob Rodamer et al

engaged to prepare and support the GTO for one race, the 1966 Daytona 24 Hour Continental. It was his first job of that magnitude, and the results—a finish and a fine international class win—attest to his skill and attention to detail.

Gail, Louise, Joy keeping lap times

Gail Lundberg Koontz: timer/lap keeper. Day job: IBM systems engineer, Cape Kennedy. Gail was Larry's colleague and a highly skilled computer professional, but the technology at the time offered nothing for automating race record keeping. So, she toiled the old-fashioned way, sitting in the pits with stop watches (the wind-up kind), clipboards (with sheets of paper), pencils (with erasers) and rapt attention to goings-on at trackside. It was probably not a skill she was ever able to apply elsewhere, but it was invaluable to the team in that setting.

Louise Eve: timer/lap keeper. Day job: schoolteacher. Louise was Bill Eve's mother, a long-time racing enthusiast and his biggest fan. It sometimes seemed that Louise thought the guys were all crazy, but despite that, she supplied tremendous support and enthusiasm. Like Gail, she helped keep the team informed of how fast and how far they traveled—and how to coordinate refueling and tire-change stops. Louise was imperturbable and never

seemed to mind the clamor, commotion or intensity of races. But she could be plenty annoyed if she thought she had missed a lap.

Teresa Jacobson: timer/lap keeper/caterer. Day job: fashion model/ housewife/mother. Jake Jacobson's wife, Teri, backed up the timing team, and supplied food for the hungry pit crew.

GERMAN MOTORS, WEST PALM BEACH, FLORIDA, TEAM MEMBERS:

Gerhard Menningmann: mechanic. Day job: co-owner, German Motors. Gerhard was both an entrepreneur and a master mechanic. It was he who performed much of s/n 3223 GT's preparation for the 1966 Sebring race. And after the car was stranded on the Hairpin sandbank, towed off and disqualified, it was Gerhard who would sample the now-demoted Victory Champagne and weep. "Oh, my poor, beautiful engine!" he sobbed—and had another generous slug of bubbly.

Svend Ibsen: organizer, manager. Day job: co-owner of German Motors. Svend contracted to take over preparation and delivery of s/n 3223 GT to the 1966 Sebring 12 Hours. Post-race, Svend returned the car to their shop and arranged repairs for the slightly damaged bodywork.

Spike Snyder: crew member. Day job: shop assistant at German Motors. Following repairs, young Spike, college dropout, drove s/n 3223 GT almost non-stop over the pre-interstate roads from Florida to New Jersey. He gives his spirited account of that unlikely journey in Chapter 12, "Spike Takes the Turnpike."

Malcolm "Mal" Love: artist. Day job: aerospace draftsman, Cape Kennedy, Florida. Mal was a tweedy, pipe-smoking Anglophile with a love for cars who raced an MGA in SCCA. Mal could draw anything needed with either hand and his eyes shut. He created race numbers and other livery ideas for the GTO and helped out generally. Mal's skill and imagination helped the team cover a necessary, precise aspect of race preparation that most had no aptitude for.

Jack Slottag: co-driver and sponsor. Day job: advertising executive. Jack was a long-time SCCA competitor who longed for a significant FIA racing opportunity. Having developed his very competent skills with a Lotus 23B sports car, and as director of the race driver school, Jack was a natural candidate to step up to the GTO. Pulling his weight with the team, Jack brought a certain amount of financial support, enthusiasm, good-natured humor and sustained speed. Jack was short and was partial to high-lift Italian shoes ... in which he drove race cars!

Russell Beazell: timer/co-sponsor. Day job: businessman. Russell raced a TVR Grantura in SCCA and originally signed on as a co-driver in 1966. But he was six-five and used to a some-what roomier, less-feisty car experience, so he elected to work instead as a timer/scorer with the crew. Russell contributed significantly by volunteering the wheels from his Ferrari 330

Chuck Rogers, world-class photographer

GTC 2+2 for use on the demanding Daytona high banks. Period photos show the car flashing its brilliant chrome spokes, and it will never be known to what extent Russell's wheels assured a safe, successful finish. There is no known photo of his new 330 sitting forlornly on jack-stands in the parking lot behind the pits.

Chuck Rogers: team photographer. Day job: aerospace photographer, Cape Kennedy, Florida. Chuck was an amped-up racing enthusiast with a magic eye and a trigger finger that would shame a gunman of the Old West. He documented the team's ventures with an artist's feel for the mix of people, machinery and drama.

RACE DRIVER LARRY PERKINS AND HIS FAMILY
. . . Larry Jr., Paula, wife Joy and Burgess.

Some of Chuck's racing and crew images are as good as any ever made.

Joy Perkins: Car co-owner/cheerleader. Day job: housewife/mother, Satellite Beach, Florida. Joy was a reluctant racing fan, but an enthusiastic supporter of the team effort. She had many years' involvement with the car community and much enjoyed its unorthodox denizens, social events, and victory celebrations.

Sophia: mascot. Day job: Italian actress. Over time the Ferrari gradually took on a certain

Enchanting namesake

feminine aura. The car seemed to have it all: exotic performance, voluptuous beauty, graceful responsiveness, elegance, and a tempestuous soul. The Ferrari embodied every provocative feature a thoroughly Italian race car could possess. In the spirit of naming cars, which many crews practiced, the GTO gradually earned the sobriquet "Sophia." (Coincidentally, in 1950, her namesake Sophia Loren, won the "Miss Elegance" contest in Italy, and by the 1960s she was considered by many as the hottest and most stunningly, irresistible temptress around.)

    MANDATORY CHECKLIST: The Car is ready to go out **only** after **every** item has been checked off—every time.

- Tires: condition/balance/pressures OK
- Wheels: secure & good condition
- Car stance OK
- Brakes: fluid level/pads/disks OK
- Brake linkage working
- Coolant: level/temperature/hoses OK
- Electrical system OK
- Spark plugs checked
- Distributor wiring checked
- Engine: belts tight/condition OK
- Fuel: level/pressure OK
- Oil: level/pressure/temperature OK
- Throttle linkage working
- Engine running smoothly
- Exhaust clear and dry
- Instruments OK
- Tachometer OK
- Battery: secure & condition OK
- Dash lights OK
- Driving lamps OK
- Turn signals OK
- Brake lights OK
- Stereo OK (a joke to get your attention)
- Running lights OK
- Race number lights OK
- Light covers taped or cleaned

- Glass clean & intact
- Wipers clean & in good condition
- Mirrors clean & adjusted
- Horn working (optional)
- Cup holder (oops, non-existent)
- Driver's seat tight & in good condition
- Seat belt intact & secured
- Fire extinguisher (none in the 1960s)
- Bodywork secured
- Loose objects cleared out
- Fasteners: all secured
- Radiator & vents clear
- Oil cooler clear
- Race numbers secure
- Get acquainted with other pit crews
- Have supplier, welding & machine shop phone numbers handy

Chapter 8: **Threading the Needle**

When the flag drops, the bullshit stops.

—JACK BRABHAM, 3-TIME WORLD CHAMPION

Ready for a little taste of motor racing? Imagine it's 1964 and after a couple of years of experience in lesser machinery, you have just bought your first high-performance race car.

You've prepared it and brought it to the track for your first race together. Practice is over and it's nearly time for the real thing—thirty laps on a three-mile road course, with nine turns marked off by peach baskets and hay bales. There are no safety barriers but plenty of trees, shrubs and grass lining the roadside, offering careless drivers many opportunities for some "agricultural racing."

Your car is poised on the grid, warmed up and waiting patiently for something fun to happen. Your crew anxiously fusses and frets over last-minute details, checking that all is ready, anticipating this first event as a team.

The excitement will kick off with a standing grid start. There is a cluster of cars ... a medley of classes running together. During practice you've seen some very quick drivers, and they're as eager as you to prove what hot shoes they are.

The first three colorful rows, aligned three-abreast on the grid:

A blue Cobra roadster • grey Porsche 904 • silver Ferrari GTO • purple Corvette Stingray • white Ford GT40 • green Aston Martin DB4 • black Shelby 350 • orange Sunbeam Tiger • your red Warrior V8.

Behind these is a mix of smaller cars ... Alfas, Lotuses, MGs, Triumphs ... two dozen in all, primed, gleaming in the sun.

Drivers mill about, not making eye contact. You stroll over to your car, looking as nonchalant as possible.

Spectators crowd in closer

　　They all wear sunglasses

　　　　Mmmm ... how about the blonde stunner in striped ones

The chief steward shouts an order: "Everybody ready!"

Time to climb into the driver's seat and go through a ritual:

Buckle flimsy lap belt

Double-check helmet strap and pull gloves tight

Try brake pedal for firmness

Adjust goggles one more time

Check mirrors one more time

Assure shift lever in first gear

Wiggle steering wheel; note front wheels obey

Give a "thumbs up" to the driver next to you

You check the spaces in front and to each side. You're on the third row, there are six cars in front—you decide how to thread the needle between them when the pack starts rolling. You scan the road straight ahead, mentally rehearsing the path you'll take. Turn 1 is a ninety-degree left-hander, two cars wide.

Everyone intends to be there first

Expect 300-yard mad dash

Big scramble for the apex

Bumping and shoving for sure

You'll need to stay clear

Up to now the grid activity has seemed quiet and orderly. The chief starter stands at the front of the pack with his furled green flag.

Tall older guy with lots of badges on his vest

Plenty of experience

He knows the drill

He's moving now

He twirls a finger in the air, signaling *start your engines.*

A sudden blast of sound goes up from two dozen unmuffled power plants, followed by loud *brrupp-brrupp-BRRUPPs* from all sides, as drivers rev and check their gauges—RPM, oil pressure, water temp, oil temp, fuel pressure. The starter strides across the front of the grid, pausing and pointing down each line of cars in turn.

Pretty girl in the striped shades

Covering her mouth with a long slim hand

No ring

You and the others in your line raise index fingers, giving the "ready" signal.

The starter goes to the front corner of the grid.

He unfurls his green flag, raises it overhead, stretches it with his other hand.

He pauses a bit … then he pauses a little more … the flag ripples.

He's testing for creepers

You check first gear again

Keep clutch down, revs up

A deafening wave of noise washes over you.

Everyone brings revs up; 3,000, 4,000; more.

RPMs they know will get them away in a hurry without stalling.

Your tach needle bobs up to 4,500

Water temp climbing fast

> *Too fast?*

Engines racing.

Everyone in gear.

Clutch pedals down … throw-out bearings smoking.

Gauge readings creeping up.

Overheating looms.

Don't jump … DO NOT jump!

Heart rates spike everywhere.

Tick … tick …

The flag arcs toward the ground … and all hell breaks loose.

Every driver instantly puts his foot down … hard.

A crescendo of roars, snarls, squeals, screeches split the air.

Air smelling of gasoline vapor, hot oil, burning rubber.

And sweat.

You mash the "go" pedal to the floor.

Let the clutch up quick and smooth.

Rear tires bite.

Revs drop a bit ... you keep the pedal down.

You're pushed back in the seat.

You correct for quick rear-end twitches.

Your revs hit the redline.

You slip the shifter into second.

Everything in your field of view—and behind you—is moving.

Fast ... you're across the Start/Finish line, fast.

Okaaay! ... you're on your way!

Up through the gears ... third, fourth, fifth.

Watch the revs.

Whole pack blasting down the straight.

Faster ... darting, pausing, jockeying for the first turn.

On the cam now... power kicks in ... speed rising sharply.

Your periphery shrinks.

You concentrate on a narrow window straight ahead.

Feeling hemmed in.

Careful, silver car, right front.

Glance at the mirror.

Don't need surprises from behind

Green car looming on the left.

Ideal line blocked.

Heavy traffic.

Cars front, back, sides.

You keep hands relaxed, light on the wheel.

Pick your space.

Lightly grip the shift knob.

Hole opening on the inside.

GO FOR IT

Hard on the brakes ... now.

Down to fourth ... then third.

Take the low gear ... second.

Go now.

Damn, the white Ford grabbed the spot

Lift a little.

Turn in ... pick another hole.

Apex is **here**.

Yellow car on the right.

Watch for that wheel closing in.

Trail the grey Porsche.

Your whole tiny world is in furious motion.

Lots of flying dust ... grit ... exhaust fumes.

Impossible to tell where everyone is.

Who's at the front?

Everyone fighting for space, avoiding contact ... a sure trip on a wrecker ...

Or an ambulance ride to the hospital.

OK ... you're past the apex.

Pedal down ... watch the revs.

Go wide right, onto the straight.

You're through ... very nice!

No time to reflect.

Everyone jamming toward Turn 2.

Another skirmish for the good line is building.

Cars strung out on the straight.

Leaders getting sorted.

Turn 2 action will be milder version of Turn 1.

Visibility better now

Silver GTO cruising at the front.

You're set up to gain some real time.

And get past the green Aston.

You stay focused.

Cars are running close and fast.

Corner is a sixty-degree right-hander.

Everyone gets on the brakes, bunching up again.

Another mob scene developing.

Ooops ... green car off ...on the left.

There's crowding ... debris ... maybe some bumping?

You don't look there.

Mustn't get trapped in that

You go to the inside ... wait ... *tick* ... out-brake the purple 'Vette.

Go deep ... drop into third.

You can see the sneaky line to daylight.

On the gas, watch the redline.

And zip ... thread the needle.

Only the silver car up front now

Dueling with drivers, giving no quarter.

Diving, stabbing, on the attack.

Hoorah—you're vying for the lead by the second turn.

You've never been exactly here before.

Standing grid starts are always exciting.

But this is your best.

Nice clear straight ahead!

Concentrating on the line for the next left-hander.

You touch 7,000 in fifth.... 145 mph ... moving right along.

You glance a couple of seconds ahead.

Watch for your shutoff marker.

You've pulled up some on the GTO.

His brake lights ... a quick flash ... early.

Wait ... is that a lovely thick whiff of blue smoke from his left tailpipe?

      ⊕

The eye of the needle

- The first turn on any track can accommodate two, maybe three cars abreast. During the start, most of the grid arrives at speed, trying to shoehorn twenty cars or so into that narrow slot. And the challenge unfolds in the span of perhaps three seconds. Somebody obviously has to give. But drivers are reluctant to give up even a foot or a split second; an early lead can be a valuable asset later in the race. Rolling starts are meant to allay some of the mayhem, but often they only increase the approach speeds that induce it in the first place. So on the starting lap in every sort of road racing, even to this day, we regularly see first- and second-turn scrums and chunks of hardware scattered around the landscape.

- Should anyone on the starting grid wave or signal "not ready," a hassle breaks out. The starter makes a slit throat gesture signaling everyone to shut down. The dead car(s) must be removed from the grid. Then the ritual is run through all over again. Some engines have overheated and may have trouble running. Everyone's taking a bath in sweat and unused adrenalin. A terrible pain in the ass!

Drivers' Meeting

Speedway officials call a meeting before a Daytona race. Stewards, drivers, some crew chiefs and press gather in a small grandstand behind the pits. The audience is international, but the meeting is conducted in the universal lingo of motor racing—English.

All drivers are expected to show up. It's to everyone's interest to get the latest scoop. For this race, there are 54 entries, normally with two drivers per car, so there are well over 100 people. The Chief Steward presides.

Here are some of the drivers entered—a mix of the prominent and lesser-known. Joining in are Larry Perkins and Bill Eve, entirely unrecognized outside Southeastern U.S. SCCA circles.

Anatoly Arutunoff	Jean Guichet	Ken Miles
Edgar Barth	Dan Gurney	Ulf Norinder
Lucien Bianchi	Walt Hansgen	Augie Pabst
Jo Bonnier	Hans Herrmann	David Piper
Ed Butler	Phil Hill	Pedro Rodriguez
John Cannon	Bob Holbert	Roy Salvadori
Ed Cantrell	Bob Johnson	Jo Schlesser
A.J. Foyt	Charlie Kolb	Don Wester
Mike Gammino	Herbert Linge	Cale Yarborough
Peter Gregg	Tiny Lund	Larry Perkins
Bob Grossman	Dave McDonald	Bill Eve

The drivers' meeting is intended to inform and to emphasize—inform everyone of any special conditions and emphasize the rules and regulations. For example:

"Welcome to the first championship race of the season; take care and have a great run."

"Lights-on will be at 1700 hours."

"No pushing of cars is allowed anywhere on the circuit."

"Pit road speed limit is 45 mph/72 kph. DO NOT SPEED in the pits!"

"Pit-board holders must not remain out on the front-straight grassy area."

"Remember ... three crewmen max over the wall for pit stops; drivers must not linger."

"Black flags will be strictly enforced."

"Any questions?"

"Yeah ... how about the pavement break-up at Turn 4?"

"The small spot at the apex will be marked with an orange cone."

"OK, let's go racing."

Chapter 9: "Who *Are* You Guys?"

PRIVATEER n., term derived from 18th century maritime practice; governments authorized armed private merchant ships to challenge enemy vessels crossing their paths during commercial voyages. In modern motor racing, factory teams were often augmented by qualified private competitors, who were given access to the best cars, engineering advice and logistical assistance, to improve a given marque's winning reputation.

I t was the era of privateers in big-time motor racing. Individuals with means and a racing itch acquired competitive cars and became "gentleman drivers" or hired professionals for the job. Their car seats were seemingly upholstered with $1,000 bills.

They were often successful in beating even better-funded groups and factory teams until eventually the economic balance began shifting toward the latter. The sport began to involve so much money that privateers could no longer compete at the top level. But while they lasted, those were halcyon days. Prize money was trivial. The glory and excitement were intoxicating.

With the steadily rising costs, paid sponsorship would have made sense, but at the time that was considered crass. "If you can't afford the wine, stay out of the vineyard," the saying went. It would be years before cars began to look like mobile billboards.

Running an internationally competitive race car was not a hobby. It was a small business—and a not-very-profitable one at that. The usual components were there: branding, capital assets, facilities, inventory, maintenance, cash flow, debt and tax accounting, marketing, staffing and training, travel, accommodations and subsistence, planning and logistics. But ... there were no customers.

Long-distance endurance racing also created an added demand: personnel scheduling. For 12- and 24-hour races like Sebring, Daytona and Le Mans, an adequate team was needed to cover all the bases. In the three days or so prior to the event, rigorous day and night practice inevitably brought crises, and crew response had to be immediate. During the race itself, a competent crew and lead mechanic were constantly on hand, round the clock, ready to spring into action within seconds to fix anything that broke, quit running or fell off the car.

It was a demanding scene in which a small team owner was usually the chief administrator, operations manager, financial officer, salesman and conflict mediator. When the owner was also one of the drivers, the challenges were nearly insurmountable. But when it's was all over … ahhhh … the rewards were delicious!

By contrast, amateur "club racing" was popular everywhere in America. A motivated, physically fit person could buy a suitable car (or even a "heap"), attend three driver schools, earn a competition license and have a fabulous time. The rewards included a feeling of mastery over a difficult endeavor, a boost in self-confidence and camaraderie for the whole family. It could be done by spending only a little more than that required by ordinary hobbies like, say, yachting or raising thoroughbreds.

In the USA, the channel for this pursuit was the Sports Car Club of America. Larry was a committed, fairly successful participant in the SCCA amateur ranks. He understood that moving into the wider sphere would be hugely different from his prior experience. He had a young family, limited means and little leisure time. Putting together another competitive car and a team to run in a league with experienced pros and privateers, on the international circuit, had seemed a fantasy until that conversation the previous fall with his cronies at the Surf bar. The temptation to drive himself nuts seemed to friends like part of Larry's temperament. He might have been threatened with "burnout" except that the term wouldn't be invented for another decade.

So it was that BARF was formed. The new little team tried all sorts of innovations to gain advantage. At one race Tungsol supplied the latest and greatest—a transistor ignition system that would light up frigid N55R spark plugs, without first resorting to N3 warm-up plugs, and produced a hot, perfectly timed spark. Unfortunately, during a practice session the system blew up and melted down, dripping molten solder and filling the cockpit with blue fumes, nearly asphyxiating the driver … Larry himself. Tungsol offered several other units, but the stewards declared them all illegal, so the crew was forced to reinstall conventional ignition.

They acquired, at great expense, an assortment of non-quick-change rear-end gears that required laborious switching for each track. Each ratio was denoted by the number of teeth on the pinion and ring gear, respectively (rated speeds being calculated at 7500 rpm with Dunlop R5 racing tires):

- 7:34 = top speed about 135 mph; suited for short courses with many turns
- 8:32 = top speed about 165 mph; for medium-length road courses like Sebring
- 9:32 = top speed about 190 mph; required for high-speed circuits like Daytona and Le Mans having long, very fast straights

They attempted in-car communications with the pits via CB radio (the antenna can just be seen protruding from the rear window in the 1964 Daytona photo). They were ahead of their time, but it didn't work; closed helmets didn't yet exist, and no one could hear anything, going either way. They abandoned that "technical breakthrough" and shut it off to allay reliability problems—the bane of any form of racing.

And then there was the problem of spare parts: they didn't have any.

Obscure but pivotal part

What is this thing? Doesn't look like much, does it? But like so many little things in racing, this two-inch gizmo can make or break a whole team effort.

It's a bushing from a ZF five-speed transmission, such as that fitted to a Ferrari 250 GTO—and only a GTO. It's exquisitely precise and utterly essential to gearbox operation. A failed part in there would be extremely bad news. One can't start a thirteen-hour race at the

Daytona Speedway or anywhere else without all the gears. But that's what happened to the BARF team during a late practice at Daytona. Third gear ceased to function, and the quick diagnosis was "bearing failure."

A frantic effort ensued: jacking up the car; dropping and disassembling the transmission. Sure enough, a bushing was burned and binding. No team in the garage stocked a replacement for this obscure part. NART boss Chinetti, still steamed over the "Al Hodges" sponsorship dispute, snubbed them.* The nearest source was the Ferrari factory in Maranello, Italy.

The race would start at 10:00 a.m. the next day. It looked like curtains for BARF's big escapade. Most teams would have called it quits and put the car on the trailer. But chief mechanic John Sabiston did not comprehend the word "quit." He just said, "We'll make one."

MAKE ONE?

"Sure. All we need," he said, "is a machine shop, a block of oil-impregnated bronze and a good machinist. In a couple of hours we'll have a nice custom-made bushing."

It's pointless to list the items they did **not** have. And it was 7 p.m. Everyone was dead tired from a day of preparation. But they set out anyhow to find a local shop at the most likely place, the airport a mile away. Miraculously, with a couple of phone calls and a short drive, they pulled up at a small, round-the-clock manufacturing facility making aircraft parts.

John showed the damaged part to the night-shift supervisor and asked whether the shop could make a replacement. But the gaffer raised a stack of obstacles; he ran a contract operation and didn't take outside orders; he had no one with the right skills; they couldn't work without drawings and specifications; he had no way to charge for the job; they might not have the right raw stock; no one was available to authorize the work ... etc.

The team put their heads together and hatched a plan: (1) they would offer the night foreman a friendly cash "donation;" (2) one of his lathe-operators would get an extended dinner break and a nice gratuity as well; (3) John would take over the lathe. In two hours, the crucial bushing would be done, and no one need be the wiser.

A deal was struck and money changed hands. The foreman showed the BARF guys where to find the coffee pot. John located suitable oil-bronze stock, addressed the vacant lathe as though he did this every day, unlimbered the bruised bushing and his personal micrometer, and the show went on the road.

A few hours later, back in the Speedway garage, the gearbox with its new hand-wrought part was back in the car. Everyone was suitably awed by Sabiston's lathe expertise. With shoulders drooping but heads up, the gang stole away to the motel for a short snooze. They would test the product tomorrow.

In a thirteen-hour race.

And so it went. BARF found themselves racing against established professional teams and actually beating several as Ferraris, Cobras, Fords and other competitors were struck down by gremlins and evil luck. Privateers that regularly ran GTOs were well recognized. But Larry's little team had come out of nowhere, and their demonstrated ingenuity and competitive potential were noted by many. It was a dream come true, but there had been plenty of tricks to learn along the way.

There were hand-made parts, e.g., the lathe-turned bronze third gear bushing and thrust washers cut from Budweiser beer cans … exactly 0.011-inch rolled steel in those days. There were unconventional substitutes, like a GMC truck throw-out bearing and Porsche light lenses and electrical parts begged from all over the paddock. A split fuel tank was nicely repaired with epoxy by a local fiberglass boat maker.

During practice for the 1966 Sebring race, Firestone was trying to break Goodyear's grip on sports car racing. They made the team an alluring offer: all needed tires and full-time engineering advice, with new compounds and combinations on the old wire wheels, free of charge. Done deal. The GTO performed on Firestone rubber like never before. S/n 3223 GT's tendency to push was gone, though the fat tires rubbed in the front wheel-wells at the notoriously tight Hairpin. Bigger rears improved grip and acceleration, though the fenders had to be "flared" with knock-off hammers to run clear when on a full fuel tank.

After three years of racing at that level, Larry was considered well experienced and was able to get rides from other privateers. He was thoroughly hooked, on both professional endurance competition and SCCA amateur racing, which he continued through 1968, driving for other teams.

Nowhere else to turn

Chassis 3223 GT, by that time dubbed "Sophia," after the gorgeous, sensual, slightly temperamental Italian film star, had seen her best days and was sold off in a very down market. But all along, Sophia had demonstrated what a marvelous racing tool the GTO was. And the team was good too; they could have made Chinetti look like an even greater Ferrari hero, if he had been supportive.

* *"We do not have advertising on Ferraris."*

So said the polite, handsome young man visiting Larry's pit after first practice for the 1964 Daytona Continental 2000 Kilometers. He was Luigi Chinetti Jr, known as "Coco," and he had the irksome assignment of informing a new-comer team that they were being protested by the prestigious North American Racing Team—NART—of which his father was *capo supremo*.

Larry's little Brevard Auto Racing Team—BARF— had arrived at the Speedway with their "new" car: a two-year-old Ferrari 250 GTO with a freshly rebuilt engine but who knew how many lurking problems. They were joining seven more GTOs in a Ferrari line-up and modestly expected to neutralize Carroll Shelby's nine Ford-propelled Cobras to win the grueling thirteen-hour race. They were a hungry SCCA-based team with big ambitions but little cash.

Emblazoned in neat white letters on the car's flanks was **"Al Hodges** Cocoa Florida." Al, a GM dealer and stock car racer, had provided generous sponsorship in exchange for a namesake promotional event. Several new Pontiac GTOs had been snapped up by eager customers, and everyone was happy ... except the Ferrari "gentleman driver" cohort at Daytona. When Larry proposed that NART recompense Hodges and he would remove the ad, they scoffed.

Bill France, the NASCAR founder and Speedway owner, was a friend, so Larry made a personal plea to him as final arbiter in the dispute. Bill was a big friendly slow-talking Southern fellow, very reasonable and easy to get along with. His response was:

"Well, Perk, here's how I see it, real simple. They didn't sponsor you, but Al did. You and Al have both run here before. Some of them haven't. It's your car, it's my track, and you and Al are my friends. I think you should run and let 'em fret over it. Best of luck."

The GTO with the dreaded advert did run, finishing eleventh in the first Daytona thirteen-hour race. So, BARF won their battle but lost the war. NART and the gentlemen's club saw to it that in three years of campaigning they could never join the brotherhood. Larry was never able to get spare parts from any conventional Ferrari source anywhere. Other privateers, needless to say, had no such problems.

Giving Luigi Chinetti his due, he had no way of knowing that, on a scale of one to ten, the BARF team considered Al Hodges' support a twenty-five.

It may have also been about honor. He had put his word on the line with Enzo that this outsider, this working stiff from Rocketville with no known pedigree, was going to be OK in the ranks of the quick and well-to-do and would comport himself accordingly. Then the guy showed up at his first outing with sponsorship adorning a Ferrari GT Car. And the sponsor was, of all things, an obscure small-town Pontiac dealer. Just not done, is it? And what would the boss back in Emilia Romagna think?

Luigi may have concluded that a way to overcome this treachery was to get rid of the guy. He knew from long experience how hard it was to run big endurance races, keep a car competitive, just keep it on the track—and how much hard cash that all took. So, he elected to shut off the supply chain for parts and technical assistance.

He probably reckoned the team of rocket engineers and SCCAers were just beginners at the Big Game. Without support, they would drop by the wayside before nightfall of their first race. But he reckoned without taking into account the resourcefulness and ingenuity of that little band. They kept entering races—and finishing with reasonable, sometimes stellar, results.

There were triumphs: a bit of prize money; some trophies; a Daytona 24 Hour class win. In one notable practice session, Bill Eve had tucked in behind World Champion Ferrari driver Phil Hill in his NART GTO Series II and stayed there, for lap after lap. He exceeded the team's conservative redline but learned precisely where it should be set … 2,000 rpm higher! An intrigued Hill visited their pit afterward, looked around and asked, "Who *ARE* you guys?!"

The little team took this question to be the Supreme Compliment.

Chapter 10: **Great Balls Of Fire!!**

Memory: A blazing fireball was racing into the stands—
headed straight at me—so I fled in a panic.
—**PETRA PERKINS**

High-pitched engines shriek by, one after another, in endless, killing, head-splitting noise. It's March 1964, nighttime. Sebring, Florida. I want to escape, run back to the parking lot, hide out in the station wagon I came in. This is torture; I cannot get excited watching cars go around and around, so boring to me, a fifteen-year-old. Here are scads of race fans, maybe thousands swigging bottles of beer or Coca-Cola, stacked at fences lining the track. Stadium lights are blinding; loud-speaker voices are deafening. The announcer is yelling like his pants are on fire, describing who's in the lead, who's overtaking, who's just skidded into the hay bales. Collective groans and alternate cheers. Mostly men, everywhere—in the stands or milling around, in race car pits, food huts, jumping onto the track, signaling with flags. Drivers fly toward the corners, jamming their brakes, popping their engines, making me cover my ears. How I *don't* want to be here; I don't understand why this is considered "fun." My Aunt Ruth brought me here because I'm visiting from Colorado and she needs an event to entertain both me and her son, George. She says "Girl, nothing's more exciting than a car race!"

I'd rather spend the evening in the Sebring library, Aunt Ruth. Loud noise is anathema to me. Cars are okay but … these look and sound like angry neon bees—taxicab yellows, bright reds and blues, ripe lime greens—zooming by us, screeching at the corner, revving up for the straight (that's what my cousin George says, and "Don't you know *anything*?") Racetrack dust spirals in the high-beam glare of spotlights. I can't even see the whole track as we're near an end which, I decide, makes it even more boring. I *don't* know anything; I just don't get it. I feel as if I should be a boy to enjoy this.

Perhaps noticing I'm a bit droopy, Aunt Ruth escalates a contrived excitement level by whooping and hollering at her favorite driver: "GO! GO, A.J.!" she yells as he charges by in a blue car. She's bought me and George some popcorn and a couple of root beer floats. The treats raise my spirits. I try to get into the spirit of this "endurance race" by doing more than just enduring it. I place my allegiance and winner hopes on one of the cherry-est red cars because they're the neatest. I pick out a number. I watch #82 go around, around, around. 82, 82, 82 …

I wince from an especially jarring noise right in front of me, a series of ear-shattering thuds and blasts. I don't see the source, but I hear it. It rocks my subconscious but doesn't register because I'm clueless. Maybe I'm thinking this is supposed to happen, so little do I know about car races.

It's early spring in Florida, but we're sweating like it's a July night of fireworks. It takes my hot teenaged exhaust-filled brain several seconds to process the fact of actual *fire* coming directly in front of me. Orange flames are leaping from the track, getting bigger and moving fast … but time and I seem to stand still, making a memory. Then, I'm awake, running in a surge of spectators clamoring to get out of the bleachers. I'm being chased by a spinning fireball. The underlying buzzing-bee noise continues as cars speed forward, swerving around fellow drivers who have crashed. Someone is burning. On top of that is screaming. Everyone scatters; I am lost from Aunt Ruth and George in the frenzy.

Miraculously, we find each other in our parking lot amid flashing lights, wailing sirens of ambulances and fire trucks that rush into the area. We leave immediately and beat the outgoing traffic. I'm relieved to be out of there and make a mental note that I will never again—*never again, as long as I live*—go to a car race.

Thirty years later. It's 1994 and I am at a car race. I'm living in Seattle and have been married three years to Larry Perkins. I overhear him talking about an experience he'd had as a race car driver, in his Ferrari GTO. Although he has occasionally told me stories about his racing days of the Sixties, they are formless to me. Surreal. I don't connect him with that era, that role, or with race cars at all. I know him as my sailboat mate, my lover, my bicycling partner, a rocket scientist, an exciting raconteur, a visual artist. A man who erupts into frequent fits of laughter. An intense highway driver who tailgates and passes others triumphantly. I don't know anything about any risk-taking race car driver, or even what a Ferrari *is,* much less a GTO.

Trying hard to relate, I surprise myself. And him.

Me: I went to a race once, in Florida. When I was fourteen, fifteen. There was a fire.

He: Where was the race?

Me: Sebring, I think. My aunt took me there.

I describe the fire and how everyone stampeded.

He: (incredulously) It was 1964. I ran that race. With Bill Eve, my co-driver.

Me: In a *red* car? (All I knew, from old photos, was that one of his race cars was red.)

He: Yep ... it was real scary.

Me: What number was your car?

He: #82.

Larry gives me background on that spectacular blaze—one that got lots of attention then, and sometimes still does. Near the end of the twelve-hour race, on the main straight across the track from Aunt Ruth, George and me, a big snarling Shelby Cobra ran point-blank into a "delicate little Alfa Romeo." A roar of engines, a quick brakes-tire-chirp and ... **WHUMP** ... right into the Alfa's gas tank, lighting up the whole night sky.

The Cobra (Dan Gurney's and Bob Johnson's) flipped end over end up the track, landing on its top and bending the car something awful. Bob, the driver, miraculously walked away with just a broken nose. "He could have died," says Larry. The Alfa was a mess, having exploded into flames, burning to the ground with the driver inside. Quick action by a rival team member from the nearby pits pulled him out and saved his life.

It was officially a racing accident, but Larry thinks it was an avoidable one. The Alfa driver had car trouble and was barely putt-putting along, slowing to (illegally) turn directly into his pit. There was no way Bob, coming up at 140 mph in the dark, could see that Alfa sitting in his path.

My family and I had been in the dark, too, and hadn't seen these details. There wasn't

A tragedy averted

much lighting at the track. The drivers could only see what their headlights picked out. But that fire really lit up the landscape.

And fire safety wasn't that good either. Racers wore cotton suits, and Italian drivers often sported nice short-sleeved polo shirts. Everyone involved in the disaster recovered, and the rescuer, a guy named Jocko Maggiacomo who also had burns, was later given a heroism award. The Alfa driver—Consalvo Senesi—opted never to race again, living to the ripe old age of eighty-seven.

So where was Larry in all this? Well, his car—a Ferrari 250 GTO—had paused in the pits with an electrical problem. When the crash came, all hell broke loose, with wild-eyed people yelling … jumping over the pit wall … running toward the fire … (unlike us, running *away* from it). Larry and his crew started shoving people aside and spraying them with a hose. Just a few yards from the fire, there was plenty of flammable stuff scattered around—gasoline, grease, oil, brake fluid, rags, rubber—with the risk of a big flash-over. Larry described the whole thing as a "very hairy scary berzerka."

The race ended an hour or so later, and everyone packed up to go home. The tragedy had ruined the day for many, but not for Larry's team—they had just finished their first "real Sebring" and the result was: Car #82, Ferrari 250 GTO (s/n 3223 GT), L. Perkins/W. Eve, 27th Overall, 3rd in Class. The silver cup from that incredible long-ago event sits proudly on a shelf in his office.

This flashback memory of Sebring gave me goose bumps. It turns out, astonishingly, that the first time I saw Larry and his red car, I was a pimply high school student, and he was thirty-one, a hotshot race driver who was pedal-to-the-metal all the way, just like he is now. He had one of the most dominant racecars available in the '60s. Today, owing to the unique dynamics of vintage car collecting, it has become a supremely valuable example.

Before Larry and me—before I had the remotest notion of "car love"—this man and machine had merged in a synergy I could not begin to fathom. When the jolting memory of 1964 popped up three decades later, I still knew and cared little about racing. I had no concept of The Car, its popularity, its mystique or why it was revered. Why are there thousands of photos of this thing? How can millions of words be written about a single automobile?

I knew even less about race car *drivers,* who had their own mystique. They appeared to be the sexiest, most charismatic of competitive high-risk takers, with unflinching boldness and confidence. It would take years to comprehend that I had married one. Within minutes of our meeting, this rather supernatural man had hypnotized me—just like a shiny red Ferrari hypnotizes and then drives one to distraction.

Driver switch - Larry out, Bill in

Stopping is the Pits

Pit stops can be choreographed things of beauty, or they can turn into frantic nightmares. But they are part of the game. In endurance racing, they can make or break a team as there are so many and long-distance racing puts such wicked demands on people and equipment.

Like everything else in the sport, pit stops are about precision and time. Precision, because a wrong move can literally be deadly. Time, because that's the essence of racing in the first place.

If a typical lap-time at a given track is, say, in the three-minute range, then any pitstop—entering, standing still for service, and leaving the pit—will lose a serious part of one or more laps on the track. A team always wants to lose as little time as possible in the pits.

1960s pit stop rules allowed no more than three men over the wall at a time (drivers did not normally work on the cars; there were no female pit crews). No assisting crewmember could sit or stand on the wall. The car's fluid covers (fuel, oil, coolant) could be unsealed and resealed only by the pit stewards hovering, you hoped, nearby. No in-car hydraulic jacks existed, so manual snap-jacks were used.

Wheels were secured with brute-force knock-off hubs. At Daytona specifically, teams were required to use NASCAR ten-gallon refueling cans rather than over-head rigs with hoses. Those specially vented cans weighed seventy pounds full and could be dumped in about twelve seconds. Planned pit stops were intense, physically demanding episodes occurring every two or three hours.

Here's a trouble-free example for a Ferrari GTO at a Daytona 2000 Km race—changing drivers; checking oil; cleaning the windscreen lights and glass; filling the 34-gallon fuel tank; and taking on two fresh tires:

- Traversing pit road at a crawl: **20 secs**.
- Steward cutting seals: **15 secs**.
- Refueling, three cans, one brawny crewman: **60 secs**.

- Operating snap-jack, twice, one man: 40 secs.

- Changing tires, two men: 60 secs.

- Checking oil level, one man: 15 secs.

- Wiping glass and checking entire car visually, one man: 30 secs.

- Steward replacing seals: 20 secs.

- Drivers switching: 30 secs.

- Exiting pit road, seeming to take forever: 20 secs.

Total, allowing for overlapping tasks and no mishaps = 2 mins. 20 secs., or at least one lost circuit of the track.

Problems would extend the agony. A failed generator, experienced by Larry's team in 1964, took twenty-five minutes to replace with an alternator. That was simply too much to make up, dropping them from fifth overall at 8:00 p.m. to eleventh at the 11:00 p.m. finish.

Chapter 11: **The Ecstasy and the Agony**

*If you want to win anything—a race, yourself, your life—
you have to go a little berserk.*

—GEORGE A. SHEEHAN, AUTHOR

THE ECSTASY

Sophia and Larry were still an item in 1965, but their affair was not going well. The year began with mechanic Sabiston needing to have either a race prep in progress or banish her from his New York garage space. There was no money to run big races, so Larry had the car air-freighted to Orlando and drove it on the highway to his home, on the coast near Cocoa Beach. He did minor repairs and installed a removable electric cooling fan for traveling on the road. He did not have a suitable trailer rig, so he again drove the GTO to a couple of regional events. But those were just long, hot, noisy, bumpy Sunday outings as there was hardly anyone in its class to compete against.

Larry was reluctant to dump the steadfast Sophia. She didn't cost much in upkeep: she wasn't registered and was not insurable. He was convinced she could still be a viable competitor in the right situation. But Larry was busy at his day job and with racing his Cooper as well as driving other people's cars. He discussed the prospects with others but couldn't find the time or money to organize and fund a major effort, like a possible entry at Le Mans.

He signed on with an old prep school roommate, David McLain, and they drove McLain's beautiful Porsche SC to 11th Overall and first-in-class at the 1965 Daytona Continental 2000 Kilometer race. David's gifted mechanic, Peter Espenlaub, proved once again that the way to victory on these long runs was to have the right guy wielding the wrenches.

Sophia, the hot Italian lady (a.k.a. s/n 3223 GT) sat at home, in a funk.

Toward year's end, though, things changed. Daytona announced the first 24 Hour race, scheduled for February 1966. Several drivers came around, offering to buy a ride in the locally available, certifiably competitive car for such an event. S/n 3223 GT was popular again.

A Florida SCCA group headed by Jack Slottag, an experienced Lotus 23B driver, and Russell Beazell, who ran a TVR Grantura, teamed up with Larry for Daytona and Sebring in a two-race, three-driver package. But there was a catch. Jack and Russell had long shared a trusted mechanic—John Brooks—who was competent but had no Ferrari or endurance race experience. For Larry and his established crew, it was to become a teaching experience.

Brooks was located in Fort Myers, Florida, two hundred miles from Team BARF's territory. On weekends, Larry and his crew, Ken Jeffers, Bob Rodamer and Jake Jacobsen, would drive down to Brooks's garage and help prepare the car, handling tasks that didn't need a mechanic's full expertise. John Brooks concentrated on the engine and drive train and supervised the work. With this collaborative effort, the car was nicely prepared, painted with new livery and delivered to the Speedway in excellent running order.

Russell Beazell, who was used to the tamer performance of his TVR, and was also quite tall, found himself uncomfortable with the GTO, and after practice laps, he elected to sit out the race. His loan of wheels from his Ferrari 330 2 + 2 road car filled out the complement of rubber and provided a safety margin during the race. The group had seen firsthand two years before what could happen with a collapsing wheel on the high banking at Daytona. They found four new wire-wheels very reassuring.

Daytona's 24-Hour race was inaugurated as the Ford-Ferrari feud was seriously heating up. It was a factory-based competition for the prestigious World Sportscar Championship, and Ford was intensely determined to unseat Ferrari from its dominance of the International Manufacturers' category. Both companies brought all their big guns; those that built the cars, their stars behind the wheel and expert race management that could make the difference. Much has been written and a movie, *Ford vs. Ferrari,* made about this fight, but the balance of power at the racetrack was clear to every participant.

Ford spent untold amounts on creating a winning car from scratch—the seven-liter Ford GT40 Mk II—and lining up a stable of the fastest, most reliable drivers available, plus engaging ex-F1 driver and entrepreneur Carroll Shelby, of Cobra fame, to orchestrate the multi-year effort. Shelby the leader and Ken Miles the engineer were together the spark

Daytona 24 Hours, February 1966. Left to right: Larry Perkins, Peter Revson, Hans Herrmann

plugs, present everywhere, every minute, making the juggernaut run. The Ford cohort embodied a noted phrase from NASA's Gene Kranz, "Failure is not an option."

Shel rolled in three Mk IIs and two semi-trailer loads of spare parts and assemblies: engines, gear boxes, rear-ends, axles, brakes and a forklift to handle them. There was even a mobile machine shop. Homan & Moody brought two more Mk IIs. The driver lineup included Bruce McLaren, Chris Amon, Mark Donahue, Walt Hansgen, Dan Gurney, Jerry Grant, Richie Ginther, Ronnie Bucknum, Lloyd Ruby and Ken Miles himself.

As a much smaller, perhaps more confident manufacturer, Ferrari was represented by three evolutionary four-liter cars—a 330 P and two 365 P2s—and years of experience with winning records. But their "silver bullet," a 330 P3, was still in Maranello being readied for

Sebring the following month, and their premier driver, John Surtees, was still recovering from a severe accident the previous year. The Ferrari entrants were all privateers, including Luigi Chinetti's works-surrogate, North American Racing Team (NART). Drivers, with the exception of Pedro Rodriguez and Mario Andretti, were somewhat lower profile: Lucien Bianchi, Jean Buerlys, Gerald van Ophem, Buck Fulp, Bill Rutan, Bruce Jennings.

The Fords prevailed. Four Mk IIs finished in the top five places. Rodriguez/Andretti managed to bring home their Ferrari 365 P2 in fourth spot. The carnage from this race was severe, with twenty-six cars out of 59 starters failing to finish. This included a mix of seven Ferrari 250 LMs and P cars and three Fords, including a Holman & Moody Mk II.

But several Ferrari privateers had better luck, and Larry's BARF team was among them. Larry, by now a more conservative competitor, had elected to bring John Sabiston in from New York as a back-up mechanic during the race. This turned out fortuitously when, during a late-night pit stop the engine refused to restart. John stepped in, diagnosed the illness, and adjusted all twenty-four valves on the sizzling-hot motor in a mere twenty minutes. Many laps had been lost but they were back in the fray.

Fuel facts: Everyone is familiar with gas stations. When one notes a low fuel gauge, one pulls into a gas pump and fills up with 10 or 20 gallons. At a racetrack, there aren't any gas pumps. Every team has to manage its own consumption, refueling equipment and procedures. And in a twenty-four-hour run, plus pre-race practice, that could be a logistical challenge.

A Ferrari 250 GTO at racing speeds used fuel at a rate of about 9.5 gals/hr (8 mpg), requiring a thirty-gallon fill-up roughly every seventy-five laps, or three hours. This established the length of a driver's stint, and the amount of fuel needed on hand at a pit stop. It also dictated the minimum number of stops during the race; seven, assuming a start on a full thirty-four-gallon tank and arriving at the finish running on fumes.

With a mandated limit of three crew members "over the wall," refueling, tire changes and other service took three minutes or more per stop. (Sometimes a pit steward wasn't nearby to cut the filler cap seal and install a new one.) But gone were the unwieldy NASCAR dump cans; the team's overhead refueling rig—a fifty-five-gallon drum fitted with a big hose—was adequate for a single stop. But it needed topping up before the next one.

Thus, roughly 400 gallons were needed by the BARF team, for their single car, for practice and the race. The Speedway provided a roving Pure Oil/Union 76 tanker truck behind the pits, and the crew was poised to flag it down whenever necessary, ensuring that they never ran out of gas. The Speedway generously provided two free items: racing gas and a second cup of coffee in the paddock cafeteria.

It was their first twenty-four-hour race. The weather cooperated, cold but dry. The experienced crew was alert and efficient. Drivers Larry and Jack kept up a quick, steady pace around the clock, thanks in part to small doses of "speed"* to keep them sharp. The brakes and Goodyear Blue Streak tires worked beautifully. And, despite that seemingly endless pit stop, they completed 541 laps, covering 2062 miles during twenty-four hours, for an average of 85.1 mph. They finished 19th overall and won the Sport 3000 class, the last significant FIA trophy for any Ferrari 250 GTO.

The team was ecstatic. The car was aging but had held up well. The crew worked smoothly together and gained valuable experience they were later able to turn into opportunity. Visiting drivers from overseas arrived at the big Florida races with cars but few other resources. They lacked familiarity with the area and had no pit crews for the races themselves. They found the erstwhile BARF Boys were capable of expert support and

Larry in early Hinchman NOMEX suit

available for hire, and the team took advantage of this in subsequent race seasons.

But on that day, February 6, 1966, no one on Earth could have predicted that many years hence, Ferrari 250 GTO s/n 3223 GT would uphold its destiny again. First of the breed. Still enjoying the limelight. Sensational!

Speed - n. slang for amphetamine tablets; taken to enhance alertness and avoid sleep; uppers, dexies, black & whites, bennies

⊕   ⊕   ⊕

THE AGONY

Sebring, March 1966: the team strategy changed again. Svend Ibsen and Gerhard Menningmann, owners of German Motors, were chosen to ready the car and support the crew at the track. Larry quickly turned the care and feeding of the GTO over to their excellent shop in West Palm Beach, Florida, and adopted a hands-off attitude. They knew exactly what was needed and prepared the car thoroughly. The Ferrari arrived at the daunting old track race-ready, with a rebuilt engine, in preeminent shape.

With heavy support from Firestone, the team switched to larger, higher-performance tires and a different chassis setup, much improving on-track behavior. Gerhard's engine was a pleasure, revving smoothly and strongly everywhere on the course. Russell did not drive, but Larry and Jack achieved respectable qualifying times with Sophia, a mature (four-year-old!) lady. Spectators began to cheer her on and make the old girl a crowd favorite.

Before the race, there had been a small controversy in the BARF team: To better accommodate heeling-and-toeing, the team had modified the car's accelerator pedal. Jack had trouble with it, owing to his dress loafers with modish Italian heels and internal lifts. The recommended style was a lightweight leather-soled shoe with a very low heel or none at all. (In those years, modern Nomex-lined driving shoes did not yet exist.) The team suggested different shoes, but Jack had only oily, rubber-soled tennis shoes, a no-no in the searing hot footwell. He had tried them during practice; his feet slipped on the pedals and the heat caused intolerable foot pain. The team then suggested removing the Gucci heels, but Jack would not even consider it. So, he drove with the snazzy shoes, lifting his heel and pointing his right toe, like a ballerina on the brakes.

Race day: Jack, Gucci-shod, won the coin-toss and took the start, getting off in the

Sebring ca. 1964-66

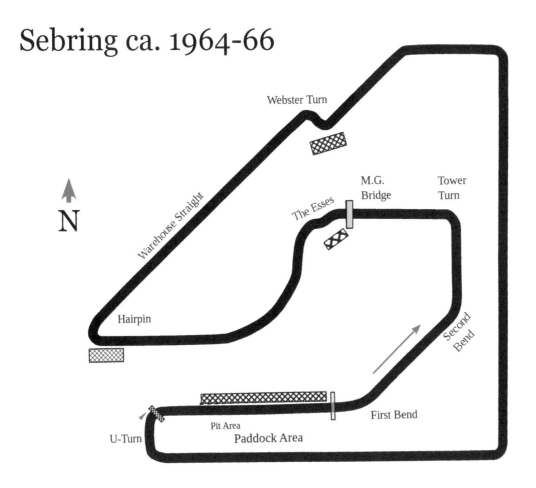

middle of the pack. Despite some slow laps, he made fair progress for the first two hours or so, then pitted for service and the driver change. In those days there were typically only two drivers. Larry, fired up, jumped in, popped the GTO in gear and streaked away. All was looking rosy for Team BARF.

At the second driver change, near the halfway point, Larry came in and warned Jack of BOILING brake fluid and a low pedal. The binders were sure to fade for a few turns until they got some air on them. He *must* be extra cautious when heeling-and-toeing for the slow corners.

Well, Jack, excited and in a huge hurry, nodded, leaped in, zoomed away ... and six turns later, "beached" the GTO high on the sandbank at the slowest corner in endurance racing, the notorious Sebring Hairpin.

Poor guy; his fancy loafer heel had betrayed him on that modified gas pedal. While downshifting from fifth gear in the Big Bend, all the way to second for that 20-mph corner, he'd been frantically trying to STOP and GO at the same time!

Jack got out to do a walk-around and check the situation. Standing by the car, he looked back up the track where he had failed to slow down enough to make the corner. Cars were coming out of Big Bend and down the straight, at 150 mph, aimed right at his soft little body. Almost surely his thought was, "What if one of those guys has brake fade? Or one makes the same mistake I just did? And they come charging up here on the sand with *ME*?"

Just then he was startled to watch, no more than 400 yards away, a Ford GT40 catapult high into the air and slam down beside the track, engulfed in flame. That sealed it.

Larry threatening Andretti for the lead ... Hah, hah

Jack knew his Ferrari was lightly damaged and could probably be dug out and made to continue. But he considered his predicament and called for a tow truck; the car was immediately DQ'd. Larry and the team were not amused.

The GTO crew had been on edge, having watched from the pits as a column of forbidding black smoke rose over the Hairpin area and having heard the track announcer say, "The GTO is off, in the sand." Nonetheless, they readied a dig-out kit—plywood slab, entrenching tool, length of rope—for Larry to carry to the site. (The regulations allowed one co-driver to replace a current driver and try to free a stranded car using hand-carried tools.) He was just setting out for a long hike when the tow truck appeared behind the pit, with Jack perched, waving, beside the dented Ferrari.

Larry caved in to his temper and his utter frustration.

"What the hell are you **DOING**, Jack? I can **SEE** the goddam car's bent. But the sonofabitch'll still **run**, dammit! We were climbing the charts, man! We could bang out that fender. This is stupid, Jack. This is **bullshit**! Now we're out! Damn! **DAMN!**"

Jack had excuses about the constant danger and the big crash he'd watched, but there was no good answer. He offered apologies, and the crew made sure to keep the guys apart. After all it was a "racing accident," which happens all the time. Still, several weeks passed before civil communications between the two resumed. And there was the little matter of repair costs to be settled. The air, and the damages, were cleared up, but the topic of the crash and those idiotic shoes would arise between Jack and Larry for many years.

The crowd audibly commiserated. The team sadly drank its celebratory champagne. Gerhard wept over the waste of his "beautiful motor." Poor Sophia, the sultry Italian, sat forlornly on the trailer, her day's run over and her career on hold. They all, including a young crew member named Spike Snyder, finally packed and went home.

As for the ongoing Ford vs. Ferrari battle, Ford took it all in a walkaway. Daytona winners Ken Miles and Lloyd Ruby, driving a new GT40 variant, the Mk II/X-1 roadster, won the Sebring 12 Hours. Walt Hansgen and Mark Donahue in a Holman & Moody Mk II took second, with the Peter Revson/Skip Scott GT40 Mk I running third.

Ferrari as a whole did not fare well. A lone 330 P3 in the otherwise capable hands of Englishman Mike Parkes and American Bob Bondurant DNF'd with a broken gearbox in the late hours. Two more 330 P3s were entered but never arrived. The sole NART 365 P2 of Pedro Rodriguez/Mario Andretti was involved in the appalling crash at the Webster turn and later burned to the ground in the pits. The best Ferrari finish was fifth for a SEFAC works-entered two-liter Dino of Ludovico Scarfiotti and Lorenzo Bandini.

Jack Slottag's stylish loafers, it later developed, were a prized personal gift from his charming young girlfriend, Seelie. She had evidently dropped a month's salary for them, and when she heard on the night before the race about the crew's "heel solution," she laid down the law. Jack could choose between possessing her, the enchanting Seelie, or letting them cobble up those lovely Guccis.

Oh, gentle reader, what would you have done?

Right … that's just what Jack did too!

Note: Sebring 1966 was marred as well by genuine tragedies. Accomplished Canadian driver Bob McLean was killed in the Ford GT40 crash. Four local spectators, the Edenfield family, were slaughtered by an after-dark runaway crash involving Don Wester's Porsche 906 and Mario Andretti's Ferrari.

It's the Pits

David Seilestad, Ferrari historian, puts an aspect of endurance racing in perspective that may elude most spectators. As they watch the cars pounding around, dicing for position, hour after hour, many have little insight into the *real* drama playing out … in the pits.

"I was not there at Daytona for that first one in 1966 but attended in 1975 when the 24 Hours race had been around a while. Things were not much changed then.

"While there was no rain during the 1966 24 Hours, it was very cold and ill-lighted. It did not get dark until quite late. The night was not long, but it was very dark, especially away from the pits. The sun was lighting up the sky by about 4 a.m. By that time, the remaining running cars were all somewhat sick.

"Compression was down, gearboxes were tired, everything was hot and little things were becoming big issues. Combined with the absolute necessity to keep running at near-record lap speeds, the finishing cars/crews were more like walking dead zombies.

"Every time a car entered the pits the shrilling klaxon was sounded, disturbing those who were trying to catch some sleep on a pile of tires or in the back of a pit.

"Unexpected arrivals scurried in, the drivers wide-eyed, breathless and soaked in sweat. The mechanics were harried, confused and anxious to get the car back into the fray. A 330 P caught fire due to a cracked manifold. The CO_2 may have cooled it down somewhat, but it still took 43 minutes to fix the ignition and repair the exhaust leak. Then it was back 20 minutes later with a blown wheel bearing. It was retired the second time.

"In the Ford and Ferrari camps, cars were failing so often that dead cars were being cannibalized. The mechanics were sent off to the dead car park (which was pitch dark) to remove parts. Everyone was working quickly and swinging hammers, etc. There were piercing outcries when a mechanic got his fingers in the wrong place while someone else was hitting. Try pulling off a front hub, out in a grassy enclosure with no light, working under pressure to get a car back into the race ASAP."

Larry concurs, adding: "There's a special SMELL to those pits—sweet Castrol R, pungent gasoline, choking exhaust fumes, the expensive scent of burnt rubber—a fusion of aromas surrounding the snarling, scorching cars.

"We can sense the tension; the drivers, the crews, brandishing tools, cutting stuff up, sloshing flammable liquids, tripping over tires, grunting unmentionable things at each other ... and at the sky!! David offers clues to how much sorcery mechanics are capable of ... in minutes.

"But over it all, in every race, there's this bubble—a sort of protective force-field of concentration and competence. Cars are roaring by just yards away on the straight at 140 mph. Conditions are beyond primitive: sand and dust flying, marginal lighting after dark. It's sweltering or cold, or rainy with no roofs over the pit boxes. Everything on the cars is too broiling hot to touch. The noise is beyond words. But the guys do what they need to and, voila, we're going again. Magic!"

PART **3** — FAST IS RELATIVE

Chapter 12: Spike Takes the Turnpike

Over a few months' time during 1966, s/n 3223 GT had covered about 5,500 racing and road miles. It had been spiffed up after Sebring, had run an SCCA race in September and was resting at German Motors' West Palm Beach garage. Larry was negotiating a sale back to its previous owner, Bob Grossman in New York.

In March, German Motors had brought a small crew to Sebring that included a young guy named Spike Snyder. He had worked for, and been trained by them after his college attendance in that area of Florida. He was clever and affable, and he and Larry hit it off. But Spike was a native of a far-away place called New Jersey, and his roots were calling. He was making plans to wend his way home when his and the GTO's destinies intersected.

Larry and Bob had reached an agreement, with a promise for delivery ASAP. Trouble was, keeping the promise created an expensive logistical dilemma. Larry's time was consumed by a new job assignment on a launch vehicle test project, and he was still racing, and he had also just bought a large fixer-upper house. Getting the Ferrari to Bob presented an awkward problem.

Then Spike raised his hand. He needed a "ride," any ride, home to the New Jersey/New York area, plus he was enthralled with the GTO and still harbored secret hopes of stepping in and diverting the sale to himself. For a small stipend he offered to drive the car to Grossman's; Larry felt he was totally trustworthy and competent to do it. With dealer documentation from German Motors, it should be a safe, practical trip. It *was* theoretically a GT car after all.

The following is Spike's narrative of how he alone rode Sophia, a serious race car, to the rescue under cover of night, over a thousand miles up old Route 1, before the Interstate existed. It was expected to be the last such road journey that The Car would make. Her future was veiled.

⊖   ⊖   ⊖

On February 24, 1962, Enzo Ferrari invited the world press to Maranello for the unveiling of Ferrari chassis #3223, the first GTO. Even today, that car is known as "The Press Conference Car," the first of only thirty-six GTOs, the first of arguably the most successful race car series of all time. All the money in the world would not buy it then unless Enzo gave the OK.

On that same day, February 24, 1962, my blue-collar dad invited the neighbors into our modest brick faced home in Fair Lawn, New Jersey, to proudly announce that his kid had been accepted into Economics School at a small Florida college. Even today, that boy is known as "Our Dropout Son," the least successful Econ major of all time.

Many of my Econ classmates were the gearhead "Children of Privilege" from Palm Beach, Florida, a swirling vortex of unimaginable wealth. They introduced me to high-dollar motor sports. More importantly, they taught me the only economic axiom I would ever learn in Florida: "Even the most unobtainable race car goes through a moment in time, usually triggered by the onset of its own obsolescence, when its dollar value drops to near-zero." This is a story about that moment.

By February 1966, I had pretty much abandoned my formal education to spend my time at German Motors, the BMW dealership in West Palm Beach. My new professors, Stuttgart's Gerhard Menningmann and Svend Ibsen, sold BMWs in a thinly disguised effort to finance their legendary race shop in back. There, my father's dreams for me evaporated into the rarified air of Palm Beach, filled with the scent of vegetable-based Castrol. Here were the cars I had only seen in magazines: Lotus, Elva, a Birdcage Maserati, a Ferrari Testa Rosa and, best of all, Enzo's first GTO, the ex-SF/NART, ex-Scuderia Bear, ex-Grossman GTO #3223, more than four years old and slipping gracefully to the status of "Club Racer."

Now in the hands of its fourth owner, Larry Perkins (a great guy and bona fide Ferrari privateer), #3223 began the 1966 racing season by winning its class and finishing a respectable nineteenth overall at Daytona. Together with a co-driver, Perkins now planned an unpretentious assault on the 1966 Sebring 12 Hours of Endurance, with German Motors handling the preparation and pit duties. His expectations for Sebring, with a nearly antique race car, must have been minimal. But wait.

At 10:00 a.m., March 26, 1966, I watched Florida Governor Hayden Burns drop the green flag on one of the most horrific Sebring events ever. In mid-race, approaching the Hairpin. Bob McLean's GT 40 Ford crashed and burned, taking his life. After dark, Mario Andretti in a Ferrari 365 P2 hit the Carrera 6 of Don Wester, and the resulting crash killed four spectators. Mechanical failures took out competitors in record numbers: the Hall-Sharp Chaparral, suspension the Parkes-Bondurant Ferrari, gearbox; the Gurney-Grant Ford MKll, timing chain. All this attrition had an unexpected effect on the Perkins GTO Ferrari "Club Racer." It started to win.

Well, maybe not win, but by the end of the third hour car No. 35, Ferrari #3223, had started its move up in the standings. Spirits were high as the German Motors crew made plans for the long night ahead. Driver changes; fuel stops; and upon whose mantle to put

Spike, the soapbox speed specialist, early days

the famed Alitalia Trophy; all these issues took on a new importance. Until, that is, lap 62.

On Lap 62, the Florida sand collected Ferrari #3223 and Larry's co-driver. Still, all was not lost. Inadvertent trips into the sand off Sebring's airport circuit are expected, and an experienced crew had provided the GTO with tools, including an Army Surplus entrenching tool (folding shovel). In a twelve-hour race, there is time, and provisions in the rules, for a driver to extricate his car from the grit and gravel. However, once the car is touched by any other person, you're out. For reasons unclear, a safety tow truck operator touched what seemed to be a still viable s/n 3223 GT, and its race was over.

I stayed a safe distance from the team's "post mortem" concerning the retirement of the GTO, so I can only speculate about what was said. Was there a missed signal between the driver and a corner worker? Was the car really irretrievable, or did the driver figure the shovel was more trouble than it was worth? One thing was clear. A disappointed Perkins had had enough. He would sell the Ferrari for whatever would cover the expenses of the Sebring event. The guys at German Motors told me those expenses came to Three Thousand Six Hundred Dollars.

This was my moment, the moment on which my whole life would turn. Where could I steal Three Thousand Six Hundred Dollars? Would my father believe I had saved him $3,600 by skipping my senior year in college? Doubtful. Maybe I could convince him someday that car would be worth millions? No, by this time, Dad, more than anyone, understood how little I knew about economics. Still, there had to be some way to park s/n 3223 in front of my house in Fair Lawn.

Sandbank damage to the GTO was duly repaired, and Larry chose to run it again in one smaller race, but wheeling and dealing continued too, and after some time the car threatened to disappear from my grasp. Perkins told me Bob Grossman, who raced out of Nyack, New York, might be interested in the car as Bob was a dealer and previous owner.

A true gentleman, Larry Perkins was polite enough to entertain the possibility that I might produce the needed cash. He said, "Nyack is not that far from New Jersey, and since the car will go to one of you or the other, why don't you take a few weeks and drive the GTO 1,100 miles, from Sebring to Fair Lawn?" I remember opening my mouth to say "OK," but no sound came out.

On September 9, 1966, in West Palm Beach, Florida, the kid from New Jersey turned the key on the "as raced" entrant No. 35 and drove it home. My old man never did come off the dime. I knew the car would eventually have to go back to Grossman—but not before s/n 3223 GT became a distinctive sight in the driveway of my dad's little house in Fair Lawn.

My GTO trip, which definitely should have been a gear-head kid's fantasy, turned out to be the most stress-filled hours of my life. My thought was, "Succeed and play in motor-sports for years … fail and spend your life in the hotel janitorial industry."

Anyway, I drove pretty much straight through, preferring not to attract attention, under cover of the cool nights … which benefitted the engine too, since it had no fan and ran very hot at anything under 100 mph. Daytimes I napped in truck-stop parking lots … afraid to get out of an unlockable, brightly painted race car even to pee.

The Georgia State Trooper who stopped me in the dead of the night never asked me to get out either. After a slow, 360-degree, silent inspection tour of the car, illuminated only by his spots and red lights, he sidled up to my window and said, "Y'all weren't doin' anything wrong … I just wanted a good look at your car."

I carried a faux registration card, and for years I kept it, along with the temporary (hand-dated) paper dealer's plate we used, but now I can't find them.

Beginning at the Florida/Georgia line, the clutch would simply not release, so it was easier to keep moving on the open road (timing the occasional stop lights) rather than risk stopping, then having to start in gear. I want all to know that I had driven multi-disc racing clutches before and, after this trip and despite Grossman's later complaint, I never abused #3223's clutch.

 Nor have I ever been that kid who did doughnuts in front of the high school. For that matter, I always thought that any form of violence against machinery was a mortal sin. (Again, once underway, the clutch did not slip … it just did not release.) The "never stop" plan worked fine until I got to the many toll booths of the Garden State Parkway. It was then I realized my trip would actually end earlier, in New Jersey rather than Nyack.

So, the whole deal was done well inside twenty-eight hours … using my start date, simple math will pinpoint my arrival in Fair Lawn. Once I arrived in Fair Lawn, there was no show-ing off. The car never left my garage … and in fact did not travel to McDonald's even once!

After a day or two of real sleep, I went to Fred Opert's dealership, a five-minute walk from my house, and reported to him that the Larry Perkins/German Motors GTO was pretty much undriveable but safe in my garage. Opert said he would contact Larry, Swen and Bob Grossman. A few days after that, Opert had me nurse the car to his shop, where it

Long night's journey into Fair Lawn

sat for perhaps a week or two. I remember those days well because we used to have to push #3223 out of the shop each morning ... to make room for customer cars ... and then back inside each night. (It turned out the throw-out bearing was shot.)

One day, a bunch of loud, greasy, chubby coverall guys came and crawled all over the car. As I recall, we started it for them and they inched it around the lot. They seemed very annoyed that the car couldn't be driven to Nyack. They made a noisy phone call ... then they got a trailer and took it away.

Spike Snyder thrives today in California, a half-hour's drive from the Pacific Ocean. He is still a dedicated "gearhead."

NOTE: Had the GTO been able to continue at Sebring, it would likely have sustained over 2,500 gear changes during the final six hours, many times more than its subsequent race and road trip. So, would race-number 35 have limped to the finish of the 12 Hours with a failed throw-out bearing?

Chapter 13: **The Un-Car**

What's behind you doesn't matter.

~ **ENZO FERRARI**

A s Sophia departed for her uncharted future, it seemed Larry's torrid affair with her was over. He continued for a while having good relationships with others—feisty sports cars and sleek single-seaters—but somehow it wasn't the same.

He had excellent luck, though, signing on to drive an Elva Ford Formula C owned by his former crew members Ken Jeffers, Jake Jacobson and Bob Rodamer, who had formed the Bent Arrow Racing Team (BART instead of BARF). The car and the team were flawless, and they showed outstanding performance, winning the 1968 SCCA Southeastern Division Formula C class. Bob subsequently took over driving duties and also enjoyed gratifying results with this team. (Sadly, Jake contracted ALS and ultimately succumbed to the disease in 1975.)

All was looking rosy for Larry until pesky reality intruded and his attention necessarily shifted elsewhere. Though the Apollo program was just beginning its amazing series of lunar flights, NASA's space-flight budget was being curtailed, and long-term activities at the Cape were phasing down. Larry, by then an acknowledged real-time computer system expert, was facing an IBM transfer to either Boca Raton, Florida, or Poughkeepsie, New York, with relatively less-stimulating work in the commercial sector.

Then luck dawned again in the form of an ideal job at Martin Marietta in Denver. It meant giving up racing, leaving Florida (or perhaps the Hudson Valley) behind and relocating his family in the middle of a school year. But he was exceptionally suited for the assignment, which was development of a state-of-the-art automated test system for the

Titan III launch vehicle, and living in Colorado, a dream he'd had for over ten years.

So it was done. Larry accepted the job offer, resigned from IBM ... a rare move in those days ... put the home on the market, bid his goodbyes and made the trip to Denver alone. His family stayed behind for a few months while Larry set up temporary housekeeping in a borrowed travel trailer and began his new life in the Old West.

His work was challenging, and Rocky Mountain winter recreation was a revelation. He was introduced to snow in the high country and never looked back, becoming a devoted downhill skier for the rest of his life, of course trying to outrun everyone.

The wonderful new job opportunity lasted just four months. With DoD's cancellation of the Manned Orbiting Laboratory program, Larry was faced with a layoff, an upheaval he had never experienced at IBM. But his boss came through with a project back at the Cape, and he was dispatched "home" again for a temporary stay. So he was at the Kennedy Space Center during the Apollo 11 mission. Larry, completing that assignment, then searched out a new assignment in Denver, on something called "Viking"—a program that was to change his and many others' lives. Viking's broad objective: search for evidence of life on the planet Mars. In 1970, this quest was considered by many a "mission impossible."

A powerful Viking proponent was Carl Sagan, an American astronomer, cosmologist, astrophysicist, astrobiologist, author, science popularizer, and full-time genius in astronomy and other natural sciences. Sagan opined that, "There is certainly no compelling evidence for life on Mars, but there is equally certainly no compelling evidence against it." He surmised that Mars might be an even better platform for life than Earth, because its atmosphere contained less of a certain poison gas, namely oxygen.

"Oxygen oxidizes organic compounds," Sagan went on, "It's not a good thing to have around. Because we humans breathe it, we think it's terrific. That's a provincial point of view."

Hoping to elevate the public's thought process above the "provincial," NASA's Jet Propulsion Laboratory—JPL, in Pasadena, California—initiated the Viking program to begin exploring the Martian surface. Larry's company, Martin Marietta, received contracts to build the stationary lander spacecraft, and the launch vehicle to deliver it, to a moving target 140 million miles away.

There were five spacecraft in all, including two flight-rated Landers. An exclusive workforce of scientists and technicians tackled these unique challenges:

- Most of the needed equipment and operating principles did not yet exist.

- Little was known about conditions on the Martian surface.

- Spacecraft mass limitations drove state-of-the-art innovations.

- Launch "windows" for such a mission came only every two Earth years.

- The mission would be remotely controlled from JPL.

The program progressed for six years, overcoming many seemingly insurmountable technical challenges and other bumps in the road. At last, on July 20, 1976, Viking 1, after its nine-month journey from Earth, set down gently on the mysterious sands of *Chryse Planitia,* a plain in Mars' northern hemisphere. It unbuttoned its complex array of instruments, deployed its color camera and transmitted to Earth the first-ever view from the surface of our sister planet.

Viking 2 soon followed, with equally stunning results, touching down in Utopia Planitia about 4,000 miles away on September 3, 1976. These probes, designed to operate for 90

Carl with the Mars Un-Car

days, in fact continued to transmit scientific data for a total of six years. They sent back compositions of minerals, indications of water and water ice, weather and seismic data, and wide-angle terrain photos. Some of their information continues to be used to augment discoveries by later missions. They did not, however, find indisputable evidence for life on Mars.

It was nonetheless a revolutionary accomplishment—and one that could never have been achieved without an extraordinary multi-discipline team effort. Collaborators numbering in the hundreds—ranging from managers, scientists, designers, engineers, test experts, planners and financial specialists to truck drivers and key punch operators—were highly motivated to pull off this expedition that had sparked mankind's dreams for millennia. All wanted to have a part in visiting the Red Planet. Program directors Jim Martin at JPL and Walt Lowry at MMC, with their deliberate, knowing management styles, kept the team marching together on the right path. Surviving members of that cohort, Larry among them, continue to gather periodically for pride-filled speeches and teary-eyed reunions.

Limitations of the stationary Viking platforms led to the development of robotic rovers able to explore the surface and carry sophisticated instruments, gathering data from different environments. The Mars Pathfinder program sent the first of these, the six-wheeled Sojourner, which landed on July 4, 1997. The program was managed by an accomplished woman (and friend of the Perkins family), aerospace engineer and writer Donna Shirley, whose book, *Managing Martians*, chronicles the adventures of this innovative rover team.

All in all, the USA continued to rack up checkered flags in the Space Race.

Larry's experience in large-scale computer design and operations during the Viking years led him to ask, "What next?" Like many men on demanding space programs, he had endured a divorce, and he was prepared for a career move into the new technology of wide-area networking. Reluctantly leaving aerospace, he joined a Colorado bank developing a system to provide online data base access to hundreds of financial officers, tellers and ATM machines. After two years, he accepted an offer as an overseas consultant to Massey Ferguson Ltd, a venerable company that built agricultural and earth-moving equipment, going head-to-head with Caterpillar, Ford, John Deere and other international competitors.

Based in Coventry, England, the European Data Processing department maintained multiple data centers in the UK, France, Germany and Italy. Their technical objective: create a computer network linking manufacturing, supply and sales operations across (pre-EU) borders, regulatory hurdles and cultural and language challenges. Larry was surprised to find it as complex as any rocket science job he had ever held.

He also found becoming an American expatriate nearly as hard as the new job. He had not done his homework before going abroad and was jolted to find that "our English cousins" lived, worked, played, ate, thought, and laughed very differently from us. Larry had assumed the European move would be eased by making his home in the UK. After all, he was fluent in English … wasn't he? Well, no, he found that the British spoke very differently too, and so began an effort to Anglicize his American dialect and vocabulary. (He ultimately compiled a 2400-word "translating dictionary" to surprise friends back home in the Colonies.)

Larry gradually adjusted to coping in the English Midlands, where it seemed that shops were closed half the time and people maintained their social life exclusively in pubs. He discovered that British beer, technically ale, really is served at room temperature … and those rooms can be 45° F. He found a nice house outside the city and was thus introduced to Warwickshire village life. He learned to shop for food, though not before he got boils and his hair fell out, as he subsisted for weeks on pub snacks, peanuts and beer. His close American friend, Jackie Hansen, came for a visit and stayed to marry Larry in the old village chapel and join the adventure. And they were both charmed to find that the English were sweet and patient and helpful to the cheeky, loud barbarians from the across The Pond.

Larry's work entailed regular liaison and visits to data centers in Britain and on the Continent, stitching together a fabric to serve a multinational customer base. There were also cultural stereotypes and differences in business conduct to deal with. Lingering animosities, the relics of centuries of war in those lands, were smoothed over. He enjoyed a cosmopolitan exposure that changed his world view and his life going forward. Along the way, Larry found it useful to tune up his college French and Deutsch. In Italian, though, as the once-owner of a Ferrari, he was ironically helpless.

Being a car guy at heart, Larry had to try some unfamiliar wheels. Skipping over the weird three-wheeled Reliant, he chose a tiny Austin Mini, partly because it had the basic

BMC engine he had raced in his Cooper for years. He found it easy to keep the Mini purring with just a hammer, pliers, and a screwdriver.

Larry had not altogether abandoned his interests in high-velocity enterprises. He became involved for a time with an aviation museum in the south of England that put on shows with such phenomenal WWII aircraft as the Spitfire and the Hawker Sea Fury. The latter, with a top airspeed of 460 mph, was the fastest propeller-driven combat fighter ever.

Since their village was only about 30 miles from the famed Silverstone track, the Perkinses also attended the Formula 1 British Grand Prix each year, enjoying the drama of the best drivers in the world competing head-to-head. Thus was a car guy's hunger for speed kept at bay.

Before leaving the UK, he bought a trimly-styled Porsche 924, the first of the marque's new (short-lived) front-engined sports car line. It was outfitted with all the USA requirements, including left-hand drive. So, for months, they drove the Porsche on narrow, left-laned British roads with their hearts in their mouths. But after departing the country, the 924 served them nicely for a long tour on the Continent—and performed reasonably well back home in snowy Colorado.

Funky Un-Car

After nearly three years abroad, Larry and Jackie returned home to the U.S. for the first time. Things had changed and Larry couldn't decide what to do next. He contacted his old friend and co-driver, Bill Eve, who was busy developing an unusual car, one he designed as an electric from the ground up. Bill's project needed a "gofer," someone with a technical background who could assist with documentation, test procedures, parts procurement and anything else that popped up. Larry took the job and found himself back in the car world, working on a kind of car that had never existed before.

The Electrek, developed at tiny Unique Mobility Inc., Englewood, Colorado, lived up to its corporate namesake. With a custom-built body, motor and control system, it was all-electric, carried four people in comfort and drove like a conventional car (rather than, say, a golf cart). It had adequate acceleration, a 75-mph top speed, and could travel fifty-five miles on a battery charge obtained with house current, a retractable power cord and an on-board charger. Bill and Larry even tested the car, as briskly as it could go, on the Continental Divide Race Track!

For a large promotional event in Denver, it was publicized as "The Un-Car" and generated tremendous public and corporate interest.

Unfortunately, the company CEO perished in a plane crash, and the Un-Car project died with him. (Unique Mobility survived to become UNQ and is now Danfoss Editron. It remains a sophisticated power source producer.) It would be three decades before another all-electric car would seriously emerge on the market. Tesla almost alone established the practicality of such vehicles, and they have become commonly available. They are certainly the way of the future in automotive transportation. The Un-Car could be said to have opened that frontier.

While Larry was enjoying these adventures, he sometimes thought of Sophia and what she might be doing. She didn't seem to get out much.

.

Chapter 14: **Racing in Rain**

In sailing, everything happens at six knots ...
until things go wrong, and then it's supersonic.
—LARRY PERKINS, SKIPPER

Larry and Petra met over a hot computer at an aerospace company in Denver, now Lockheed Martin, on a military communications development program. They discovered as co-workers that they communicated very well, which led to friendship, then love, then to long lunches during which Petra raced her light blue Fiat Spider 124 against his lime green Porsche 924; then to Sailing 101 on a 16-foot boat; then to a Formula One Grand Prix in Monaco, where Petra fell for Aryton Senna and Alain Prost and the luxurious yachts shining like sea jewels in Monte Carlo Harbor; then sailing on breezy Chesapeake Bay where they ran aground; then to lessons on a 40-footer in Tampa Bay; then to sailing the Ionian Sea in Greece (like the wanderer *Odysseus*); and then to buying a Hunter 25-foot fixed-keel "yacht" they learned to race in Denver regattas and named *Artemis* (twin sister of Apollo) after the Greek goddess of the moon, the hunt, wild nature and chastity. And if that wasn't romantic enough, they moved to Seattle, "The Emerald City," ending up as racers in rain.

Of course, Larry ran a "Formula One of Water" type of race—i.e., seriously serious—which knocked the socks off any casual Sunday racer in the Chatfield Lake Yacht Club who still wore socks. *How could those two possibly compete in that klunky grand touring ship? Hahaha.* Well, they did, coming in all over the charts—third, fifth and seventh place. (Okay, there were only seven boats in that last race.) If there had been "class" competitions, they would surely have won some. They never DNF'd!

Originally, Petra had this fantasy that sailing was about watching the clouds and

Petra and Larry raced to the altar - 1991

scenery go by while sipping an icy lemonade. No. It turned out that Larry needed to know every single part of the boat right away and analyze how it worked so that more *speed* could be attained. This was a revelation to Petra and soon it became apparent, if only to herself, that she would have to up her game. Neither imagined their destiny: to race this heavy cruiser, sometimes in heavy *rain,* in heavy seas, against young nautical geniuses in race-worthy speedsters.

As the wheel of life turns, sometimes serendipitously, it turns out that Bill Eve—Larry's GTO co-driver (a.k.a. Fastest Dude in the World)—lived near Denver at this time and was a sailboat racing expert! Bill, and his wife Melanie, taught Larry and Petra some boating techniques: stepping the mast, hauling the sheets, trimming the jib, and how not to flip the boat over in a blow. Bill, a regular participant in Cherry Creek regattas, also divulged some secrets to advancing a half-second past his competitors: e.g., tweak the downhaul, run goose wing downwind, rush to douse the spinnaker when rounding onto a beam reach.

The Eves had an intriguing trick for winning when there was no wind. Sitting becalmed in the middle of the lake, Melanie would light a cigarette and hold it still, letting the smoke drift upward. The tiniest, nearly undetectable breath of breeze would slightly disturb that smoke and Bill would pounce on the advantage. Concentrating on its direction, trimming, and teasing the sails ever so gently, he would catch the most miniscule hint of power in the air, and their boat would slowly, slowly inch ahead, amazing and frustrating the rest of the regatta.

So just as it was back in the '60s, it was all about winning for Bill and Larry, but always with style and finesse. Exciting afternoons were spent cheering Bill Eve (who had once kept up with Phil Hill at Daytona in 1964) as he and his sleek Santana sloop won or placed. The Eves eventually left land-locked Denver and set their sails back toward Daytona Beach to drop anchor in the Atlantic.

In Colorado Petra and Larry thought how much more fun it would be to sail on Big Water rather than just a "bathtub" of a small lake. So, the couple tied the knot matrimonially as well as sailing-wise and packed up and moved with *Artemis* to Seattle, where there were already a gazillion boats. Talk about carrying coal to Newcastle!

Petra landed an IT management job in downtown Seattle and Larry retired from aerospace to become a part-time sailor and part-time computer network consultant. On weekends they raced *Artemis* on Puget Sound, where skies can start out merely cloudy but deliver a full-on cold rainy scenario. Like most newcomers, they quickly learned that to do anything in the Pacific Northwest—hiking, biking, skiing, racing boats, even waiting for a bus—one must commit to the wet or never do anything at all.

Regattas were held rain or shine, and poor *Artemis,* lonely nomad from the high desert lake, never won, but the sailors became increasingly proficient in Big Water. They sailed from the north to the south end of Puget Sound—and got into big blows in which the boat lay practically on its side. They wore foul-weather gear and mastered life-saving man-overboard techniques. They briefly considered living aboard the sort of boat where *Sleepless in Seattle* was filmed. They even sailed their tiny sloop, one pitch-black night, right up to the monstrous aircraft carrier, the *Carl Vinson,* as it chugged majestically into Bremerton Harbor.

Artemis went from being a big fish in a small pond to being a minnow in a huge lake.

She was the tiniest sailboat to travel up and down the middle of Puget Sound dodging teeming commercial traffic. However, the sailors decided that racing a small boat fast was not really as much fun as racing a big boat faster. With a dream for double-handing a swoopy ocean-going vessel to sail across the Pacific, they took Coast Guard nautical lessons and attempted a practice run north toward Canada via the San Juan Islands. But they didn't quite make it due to torrential rain, powerful currents, and Petra's timidity. Larry, of course, wanted to go for it … full speed, at night, in the wet.

Sailboat racing was tricky to learn, as the boats hover around the start line until the shot is fired. And then whoever is closest takes the lead and decides the direction of tack. All this happens while trying not to collide. It's a bit like starting a car race as it's frantic and full of chaos, and boats come dangerously close to colliding until everything is sorted out and some spacing develops. In the rain, though, one is even more challenged by frigid spray, poor visibility and a little misery.

At one point, to escape racing in rain, Larry and Petra looked at applying to an established team for the Vic Maui sailboat race—Victoria Island, British Columbia to Hawaii, 2,300 miles across the Pacific. The draws for Larry were the challenges of sail handling and ocean navigation whereas for Petra it was survival (and enjoyment of dolphins, albatross and brilliant starlit nights). Alas, it required too much commitment away from work, so they abandoned the idea.

While they were sailing every weekend and searching for the GTO of sailboats, Larry did two unrelated things: first, he joined SOVREN, Society of Vintage (Car) Racing Enthusiasts, and second, he signed up for life drawing, sketching and sculpture lessons. The latter was to be life-changing for him.

The very first piece he sculpted for casting in bronze was a prototype of a race driver—sitting in racing position, with no car around him. The enlargement of that first bronze casting called "CASINO" was a likeness of Phil Hill in racing posture. It was a stunner that won some local art show awards and was purchased by the town of Puyallup, Washington, for permanent outdoor display. (Other copies in that edition have been placed in the U.S. and Europe). He also created a small Lotus Elise, a Ferrari Dino, an MG F and a striking bronze relief portrait of the great driver Tazio Nuvolari. Larry had never previously had art lessons or done artwork in his life, but suddenly a creative streak was unleashed. Perhaps it was the negative ions of the rain that inspired him.

Larry aboard Artemis

Although he considered investing in a vintage race car, a subject he brought up with Petra ("What color?" she asked), Larry decided to focus his time and money on becoming an artist. In Seattle he began a new career creating bronze sculptures of people doing adventuresome things. His largest figurative work was a monument to fallen firefighters, called *Fully Involved*, a life-size trio placed on the waterfront in Tacoma, Washington. Larry had been a volunteer fire engine driver (who sometimes "raced" his pumper to fires) in Colorado and it was in doing that work he became inspired to honor the ultimate sacrifice made by firefighters. By a grim coincidence, *Fully Involved* was installed just two weeks before the 9/11 disaster in which 343 firefighters were lost.

At SOVREN, Larry returned to his element of long ago. He was again immersed in the competition culture he had devoted so many years to, and he found a natural bond with the other members. Attending vintage races, he volunteered as a Technical Inspector, assuring the safety of the equipment and the racers' adherence to the regulations. He was sort of *in it* once more.

The operative word being *vintage*, it all felt to him like a journey to the past. The safety procedures were modern, requiring roll bars and extinguishers and up-to-date helmets and fire suits. But the cars ... like MGs and Triumphs and Formula Fords and Alfas and, yes, Ferraris ... were required to stay in-period. Tires, in particular, offered an interesting challenge; grippy modern tires put damaging stresses on vintage suspensions, but genuine period rubber has long-since rotted away. And the rain (except for about four or five summer weeks a year) posed dicey situations all around in races.

The best and most surprising aspect of vintage racing, to Larry, was that once behind the wheel, drivers displayed determination and commitment and grit every bit as intensely as if they were running for money and points in "real" races. The competitive urge and the *need for speed* are apparently timeless. Hmm, Larry almost changed his mind about buying a vintage car.

At a few vintage races in Seattle, Petra noticed that people would ask Larry about his GTO, but she still did not understand about its fame or why it was an important car people gushed about.

"So, you really owned a 250 GTO, that incredible car?" someone said.

"Ahh, it actually owned *me*!" Larry replied.

"And you raced it. My God, what was that like?"

"Well, it was kind of like racing a boat. In a boat you throw thousands of dollars into the water. In a race car you throw the money out the window on your way around Turn 1."

Then he would launch into some stories of his racing days, and the car guys would be enthralled and talk about engines. Petra still didn't get it—as "IT" was a long time ago, and after all, it was just a car, right? She'd yet to see "Sophia" up close and personal. (One can possibly relate by imagining the sight of Sophia Loren in the flesh, very close, not by photo.)

Chapter 15: Where in the World is Sophia?

Race it or sell it. Better yet, DON'T race it … just sell it for scrap.

—JOY PERKINS, S/N 3223 GT CO-OWNER

Old race cars seldom die. At least of old age. After enjoying a short, exciting youth, after whizzing past their last checkered flags, they slide into retirement and take up other pursuits.

Some are re-geared, re-motored and become drag racers. Some are immersed in nostalgia and continue to show their stuff in historic events or sit proudly in museums. It's rumored that one or two have been transformed into colorful numbered hot houses for cultivating weed (as opposed to *weeds*).

Larry even had a Formula Jr that he sent to a good home, only to see it chopped up and converted to a bizarre short-track midget racer with a Chevy Corvair engine. (Interestingly, that old car still exists, undergoing a restoration in New Zealand!)

Over time the thirty-six Ferrari 250 GTOs have evaded such repurposing. They became "iconic" and were absorbed into the upper echelons of classic auto collections. But, true to their Grand Touring DNA, they were eminently drivable, participated in anniversary rallies, and could still put on a startling show of velocity and agility on a vintage racetrack.

S/n 3223 GT departed Larry's garage in late 1966 and, for quite a while, he was too busy to wonder much about Sophia's whereabouts. When Larry finally became curious about what had happened to his old car, the World Wide Web did not yet exist. Sources were sketchy, so it was pretty hard to find any trace. The GTO had apparently wandered away into the wilds of the Northeastern USA.

Then, after two decades, he came across this startling *Chicago Tribune* headline:

U.S. PICKS UP QUICK CASH IN SALE OF RARE FERRARI

A rare, red 1963 Ferrari GTO owned by an alleged leader of a drug ring has been sold by the federal government for $1.6 million.

Larry's interest was suddenly piqued. GTOs were out there, He marveled at the awesome auction price. He wondered which GTO this might be. The model year indicated one of the later cars, but no chassis number or other details were included. He made a few phone calls, but no one could enlighten him. By chance, in Colorado Springs, he met Bob Donner, who showed him the last Series II GTO built, s/n 5575 GT, but Bob couldn't provide information about s/n 3223 GT. Dead end.

WHERE IN THE WORLD COULD SOPHIA BE?

It turns out she had been on an extended trip, passed along for brief stays with several admirers then to the automotive equivalent of a homeless shelter, and finally was making a long, useful recovery. The trail can be followed in accounts by noted Ferrari historians Alan Boe and Marcel Massini, but few details have been preserved from those early days, when she was passed from hand to hand with some mechanical modifications and limited exposure in racing or show competition.

From Bob Grossman's dealership in West Nyack, New York, the GTO moved on in 1967 to John Ercole and John Mastroianni in Armonk, New York. As the family remembers it, the car had sustained some minor damage which they repaired and resprayed it red with

Mastroiannis at play with 3223

a gold stripe. They had no way of knowing that the engine was relatively fresh from its short season the previous year, so they rebuilt it. This was a super opportunity for the Mastroianni boys, as the list of mechanics privileged to work on the Columbo V12 was decidedly short. The tall 8:32 diff ratio wasn't changed, and the car was driven lightly on the road and in demonstration runs at the Lime Rock racing circuit.

Sophia's dramatic plunge came in 1968 or '69, when she was acquired from the Mastroiannis by a now unnamed person, believed to be a musician with the Baltimore Symphony. This uncaring cad jilted her, in damaged condition, at curbside in the city's genteel John's Hopkins University neighborhood. She was confiscated by the traffic department and towed to the city's abandoned car impound facility.

By great good fortune an astute collector, George Sterner, of nearby York, Pennsylvania, learned of this development and was able to buy the car at auction for about $2,500 and take it home. It is conjectured that this was the lowest price ever paid for any Ferrari GTO. It's also a fair bet that at this juncture, s/n 3223 GT, the trailblazer, narrowly avoided disappearing forever in the jaws of a derelict-car crusher.

After resting comfortably for five years in the Sterner collection, the car was revived and enlivened by Dr. Robert Bodin of Minneapolis, Minnesota. Dr. Bodin recognized that she, like his other racing Ferraris—250 GT LWB TdF and 250 GT SWB—would never be a proper garage queen and deserved an active life. And he delivered on the promise, providing many thousands of miles in vintage events in the U.S. and Europe.

As historian Alan Boe has observed, "The ultimate tour ride ... has to be on board the greatest and most prized Ferrari of them all, a 250 GTO." Bob Bodin accordingly drove the GTO over the road, ran historic races, and joined anniversary tours on the Continent. He even treated Sophia to a homecoming at her birthplace in Maranello, Italy.

One of the adventures with s/n 3223 GT that Dr. Bodin reports involved a slight anomaly in the right-hand seat department. The GTO, being a grand touring car by only the slimmest interpretation, was in truth never intended to accommodate a passenger. At least not comfortably.

The seating on that side thus underwent a concession to endurance competition needs which included a nice cool placement for the over-size battery. Originally mounted in the engine bay, close to the right-side exhaust manifold stack, the battery was vulnerable to one of its most hostile enemies—sustained heat over many hours at a stretch.

The battery box under the seat was shallow and the big battery, with its heavy-duty wiring, was taller. So, it was covered with insulated padding, and the seat secured over it with bungee cord. All was secure and trouble-free, but it tilted the seat forward at an angle, just enough to keep a passenger under a strain, even for a short ride.

It was this uneasy perch that Mrs. Bodin had to maintain on a long cross-country drive from Minnesota to a race meeting at Watkins Glen, New York. Coupled with the ear-splitting noise—and the sweltering cockpit temperatures that GTOs routinely generated— it was surely a heroic performance on her part.

In 1993, David Gizzi, a California broker for exceptional cars, took charge of s/n 3223 GT. Dr. Bodin had sold her on, through Gizzi, to Japanese collector Yoshikuni Okamoto, and a certain amount of refurbishment was required before the car could be sent on its way.

Sophia ... Abandoned in the urban wilderness

David kept the car at his home in Carmel, drove it extensively in the area and arranged for its partial restoration, primarily doing a respray and adding a dash fascia where only exposed frame tubing had previously existed.

He presented it at various events where Ferrari was being honored during the 1994 Monterey Car Week—including the FCA Concours at the Hyatt and the Concorso Italiano at The Quail. When the gala was over, David arranged shipping to Mr. Okamoto in Japan.

Like so many who have "lived with" GTOs as road cars, Gizzi was surprised to find the all-out racer very Spartan but impressively tractable and only moderately hot and noisy. Gizzi reports that he experienced an incomparable year of fun just *DRIVING* the GTO. Once again, Sophia had proven that she could be a marvelous companion.

Of course, during all the ensuing years, Larry had been unaware of what was transpiring with Sophia and her suitors. He just hoped fervently she hadn't succumbed to one of those evil crushers somewhere.

3223 under Dr. Bodin's care

David Gizzi presents some of his wares

Meanwhile his new career as a sculptor was attracting him to Monterey, California, for the 1994 Car Week. This classic car extravaganza was a must for showing his first bronze, "CASINO," a vintage action-figure of a race driver.

On a hunch, Larry located and packed Sophia's original ignition key and photos of the car in her racing days. He thought, "Monterey events host hundreds of collector cars. This time it is a "Ferrari Year." Maybe, just maybe …."

Sure enough, when he approached the Ferrari Club of America about their events, he discovered there would be a Ferrari show on the green sward of the Hyatt golf course and another at The Quail Lodge south of town. There was also a multi-day classic car auction running at the convention center. Unfortunately, though, no one had any idea which specific cars were on hand. Larry still didn't know whether "his" GTO would ever surface again or be destined to make a big splash. He had to be patient until he could make the rounds. Larry had never been famous for his patience.

Chapter 16: **A Key Find**

Every parting is sweet sorrow; every reunion is a heavenly embrace.

—WILLIAM SHAKESPEARE [SORT OF]

Monterey Car Week: August 1994. As soon as Larry arrived at the oceanside city, he met Bill Patterson, an artist he'd known before, who was marketing his dramatic race paintings and themed clothing at the huge event. Bill offered him the auspices of his booths at The Quail and the Laguna Seca racetrack, perfect spots to display Larry's driver sculpture "CASINO." Larry, always gregarious, met other motor racing artists—painters, sculptors, craft makers—who all admired the big bronze, its caramel patina body and bright gold helmet shining like blazes in the sun. "That's Phil Hill!" they'd say. It stopped people in their tracks, and Larry would start talking. It wasn't long before he had a serious looker.

Larry's son, Burgess, had come along to help, and one morning he spotted a patrician-looking man circling the sculpture, looking at it intently and snapping pictures. "Dad, I think you ought to approach that guy."

Larry immediately went over, extended a hand and introduced himself.

"I'm *Pee-tah*–Peter Kauss," the prospect said with a light accent. "Pleasure to meet you."

Peter Kauss turned out to be a German car collector who owned the world's largest and most impressive museum for cars and car art: Rosso Bianco in Aschaffenburg near Frankfurt.

"I assume you'd like to sell this piece?"

"I would, yes. Would you be interested in it?"

Phil Hill Immortalized in bronze
(by Larry Perkins)

"I like it very much," Peter said, "But I prefer von Trips. Would you have a sculpture like this of Wolfgang von Trips?"

Larry must have smiled broadly, since it was Taffy von Trips himself who'd led Larry into motor racing long ago, taking him for a wild ride in a Ferrari, making him wonder if they would die. But he had also inspired Larry with his phenomenal driving skills. Taffy and Phil Hill had raced together on the Ferrari team one final time at Monza in 1961, when von Trips was killed. Before his crash, he'd been leading the Formula One World Championship race, a point ahead of Hill, when he hit Jim Clark's Lotus and flipped, dying along with 14 spectators. It was a devastating tragedy, but the race continued, as was common in those days. Hill went on to dominate the Italian Grand Prix, becoming the first American to win a World Championship. It was a sad win for Phil. Wolfgang became a lasting national icon to his German fans.

"No, I don't have a von Trips," Larry said. "But he was a personal hero of mine. I could make a sculpture like this of him."

Peter was quite enthused. They discussed how a half-life-sized likeness of Wolfgang, would be made and placed in the museum. "I'll have them both," Peter decided. "They'll be side by side, Hill and von Trips, just as they were in life."

And so, to Larry's delight, a deal was struck whereby Larry, barely starting out as a sculptor, would have a commission for not one but two large bronzes for Kauss' museum. Larry had suddenly become an international artist.

Later that day, Phil Hill came by the booth with Denise McCluggage. She had been an active '60s sports car driver (always with her distinctive helmet covered in red polka dots, long before other drivers decorated their helmets). She was also an established automotive journalist and writer, having just published her new book, *By Brooks Too Broad for*

Leaping. Denise was a legend in her time.

Phil and Denise, as well as the renowned car designer Carroll Shelby, admired the sculpture and, next day at Laguna Seca, groups from the pits came to look it over too. Jay Leno and his entourage dropped by for a chat. The glamorous celebrity stream captured the attention of Larry's son, Burgess, who was pleased to note that some "car guys" were actually very attractive women.

Larry Perkins was once again at a car event, engaging with real car people, as he had thirty years before. Only this time he was there as a participating artist. One of the participants he met was the English artist and photographer John Olliver, who specialized in motor racing and cars. John introduced Larry to noted journalist Eoin Young, a New Zealander, who had an encyclopedic knowledge of racing and an extravagant sense of humor. Both John and Eoin shared a fund of amazing first-hand stories about motoring events and people that significantly expanded Larry's horizons in the sport. John and Larry got along famously, becoming close friends, corresponding and visiting across the Pond in later years.

Larry took some time off from marketing art to visit the car displays around town. He passed vintage models of all sorts—coupes and cabriolets, road cars and race cars, cars dating from the early days of the '50s to modern times, and in many different colors. And then he chanced on It. The Car. He knew right away. He hadn't seen it in twenty-eight years, this plain red Ferrari 250 GTO, with no race numbers, and it could have been any of the other thirty-two like it, but, somehow, he knew it was the one. A man was standing close to it.

"Beautiful car. Worth a pretty penny, I suspect," Larry said. Laughing.

The man was polite when Larry said, "That *could* be my old car. I used to drive one of these."

The guy was unimpressed. "Well, there were thirty-six of them built, y'know."

"Yeah … well, actually thirty-three like this, but mine was the first one. The torch bearer."

The man chuckled then. He might as well humor this eccentric old gentleman, so he dared him. "Okay, so what makes you think it's yours?"

Larry walked over and looked in the window. "We changed that firewall mounting and put a no-slip wooden block on the clutch pedal."

The man seemed very familiar with the car; a judge maybe? He said, "Yes, um, this car has those, but that doesn't prove much."

"And we moved the battery so it wouldn't overheat. I guess you noticed—the battery was once on a bracket in the engine compartment. We moved it back to the passenger seat, where it would stay cooler."

The man now seemed *a little* taken aback. "But I still wouldn't assume it's your car." He must have thought Larry was a delusional fan who had wandered into this show by mistake.

Some other people had begun to crowd nearer and listen to the conversation. A French TV crew had shown up and began filming.

Larry said, "The brake pedal had welded pips on it; they used to make marks on my shoe sole from my mashing on it hard. And we rearranged the cooling vents to try and get some air to the driver. Any of that stuff in there?"

The guy was starting to turn slightly pink.

"Maybe. Was your car serial number 3223?" ventured the man.

"I don't have a clue. I can't remember. We called her 'Sophia'. Sold her for $3600 and I heard later she ended up abandoned in an impound lot. I never expected to see her again."

"Well, this is 3223 and *she* definitely didn't get junked, or *she* wouldn't be here, see, so … probably not yours."

The man was rightly skeptical that this GTO could've been Larry's. He couldn't imagine this old man having raced it, having lifted trophies overhead in victory.

Then Larry pulled something from his pocket. "I think this might be the tie breaker."

As he held it up, the French film crew moved in for a close-up.

"This is the original factory key. In fact, when I sold the car in '66 I gave the buyer some hardware store copies on a little leather key fob. But I kept the original, and here it is."

The judge pulled his key set from his pocket. Keys on an old leather fob.

Larry said, "That's them!" as he put on a Cheshire Cat grin. He really knew how to enjoy winning.

By then a friendly chap named David Gizzi had stepped up. He had been listening to the conversation. He explained that he brokered the deal the last time car was traded, to the current owner, a prominent Japanese collector who was in fact there at Monterey that day. David confirmed the keys on the leather fob were the ones he sold with the car.

David asked a couple of questions about the car for which Larry had ready answers.

The man with the key

Then David said, "No harm in trying it." He slipped into the driver's seat, put Larry's key in the ignition, turned and pushed it. A steady *tick, tick, tick* ... the fuel pump was running. A whiff of fresh gas. He cranked it all the way over, and .... RRRR-uuuuUUUHHH-FFFAHHHH! RRRR-uuuUUUHHH-FFFAHHHH! The venerable V12 awoke with a vengeance.

Larry, moved by that ferocious old Ferrari sound he knew and loved, couldn't stop a few tears of elation from coming.

Everyone cheered. *"Oh, mon dieu, magnifique!"* shouted the French cameraman. A few people in the crowd understood what had just happened and what it meant. Here was the guy, a lucky guy indeed, who'd raced the first-ever Ferrari 250 GTO, the flagship of the original series, probably the most notable car in this town today. And he had competed with the likes of World Champion Phil Hill, who drove one of the other 35 (5571 GT).

Larry explained to David Gizzi that he had brought photos from the 1961-66 seasons, and if the current owner would like to come see his Phil Hill sculpture ... he'd gladly make him a gift of the photos and the key. David assured him that the owner and his wife would visit Larry at the artists' booths. But apparently neither the photos nor the art, nor the key were sufficiently enticing as the collector never showed up to see them or to talk about the origins of his famed Ferrari, or to meet the man whose butt had helped shape the driver's seat in his world-class investment.

Number 3223 GT disappeared after that day, and the next time Larry and Sophia rendezvoused, seventeen years later, they would each be heading for a restoration.

Chapter 17: **Competitive, at its *Most* Superlative**

Get out in front. Stay out in front.

—A. J. FOYT

Petra reflects: I didn't understand the word "competitive" until I met two certain race car drivers. And then it was an epiphany.

The first was Larry. He started instructing me, soon after we met, on the nuances of driving a car. I was transporting an office bunch to lunch at a restaurant one day, and Larry was in the front passenger seat. We were at the beginning of a mountain road three lanes wide.

"If you take this corner in the left-hand lane and stay on the gas, and take a straight line to the right lane, you'll save a couple of seconds," he said. "Then when you get to that turn up ahead, do the same in reverse. Just ease in front of that truck, it'll be fine."

What? Swerve in and out of my lane? Clearly, I did not understand. Why should I save a couple of seconds? At that time, I didn't know much about him—that he'd been a race car driver or race driver instructor. And it was a long time before I learned this.

"Always be looking ten seconds ahead."

At the start of our friendship, I remember feeling self-conscious about every corner, acceleration, braking, passing. Self-consciousness turned into anxiety; anxiety became fear: Was I a terrible driver? No. Larry just wanted to make me a fast/better one, but I didn't see the point. I wasn't competitive. I wasn't living life in the fast lane, yet. *What's the hurry? Just enjoy the journey.* Finally, I relaxed and drove the way he suggested, most of the time, and I did wind up a smoother and even safer driver. (It worked in skiing, too, to develop more controlled speed.) Larry urged me to sign up for driving lessons at

Sears Point Raceway in California, which seemed incomprehensible, but I wished I'd done it. One time I drove a Lamborghini around a makeshift racetrack, and he tutored me in advance how to corner: Lift, Brake, Shift, Turn, Gas. Lift, Brake, Shift, Turn, Gas. I did it, roughly better each lap, and the perceived power was nothing short of a "rush." I wanted to *keep on* doing it, all day long. Finally, I could see why racing a certain car—a car that one bonds with—might be strongly addictive.

Growing up, I'd participated in occasional sports, but mostly for the fun. I didn't really understand the meaning of competitiveness (except in spelling bee competitions) until Larry and I learned a sport together—sailing, which turned into sailboat racing faster than he could haul up a spinnaker. And, as mentioned, the person who taught us to trim that spinnaker and to race our little yacht was none other than Bill Eve, Larry's former GTO co-driver, a.k.a. Fastest Dude in the World, who was known as a notorious feared contender on Colorado's lakes.

My initial idea of sailing was so sweet and utterly naïve. It was to "do a few things" like set the autopilot, sit on the bow and be lookout for pirates. I was clueless that we were going to harness every cubic inch of air to overtake another boat—a better racing boat. I didn't know we were going to grind those winches, haul those sheets, tweak those clews, and memorize books on speedy knot-tying and heavy weather sailing. But Bill knew it all. He said, "If you're going to own a sailboat and throw money in the water, you might as well race it." And, to Bill, that meant you must do everything humanly or mechanically possible to WIN. This involved absolutely no lounging or lollygagging.

Ours was not the GTO of sailboats. Ours was kind of a klunker with a heavy keel. It was like a GTO in that the GTO was called a touring car (but it really wasn't one), and the sailboat was a touring boat. However, *Artemis*, although named for a winged Greek goddess of the moon and the hunt, was never designed to race. Yet Bill and Larry turned it into a race boat. They taught me, in regattas, to hunt for that air, no matter how scant, and to convert air into power and convert power into speed. Speed was *everything* to these guys. So much for my lazy visions of lying on deck and spotting animals in the clouds.

Still, I was clueless about competitiveness, this incurable condition. I hadn't caught on about the *greed for speed*, either. I remembered when Larry and I worked together at the rocket factory. Intrinsically, he strove to be his best at every task he did, and the fastest, whereas I was pretty happy not to DNF and satisfied to merely stay within budget. There's a saying in the aerospace business—Good/Fast/Cheap: pick two. Larry always chose Good/Fast.

He was good and fast at almost everything he tried. Besides work and driving, Larry could outski me to the bottom of any hill and outhike me to the top. Outswim, outtalk, outbike, outlast. When he was in his seventies, he decided to make one of his dreams happen. Larry signed up for a one-of-its-kind foot safari through the Tsavo National Park—a jungle of wild animals—in Kenya. Although I wanted to go, I decided I couldn't handle walking and sleeping in the heat of Africa—or possibly seeing a killer snake. The scariest part of that trip turned out to be the leopard following their group as they trekked the paths of lions, hippos, and elephants and through rivers owned by crocodiles.

Clearly, I wasn't brave enough. But Larry thought nothing of fear, even though, starting out, he wasn't in tiptop physical shape. On Day One, he realized he was the oldest (out of eight) in the group and not sure he could sustain the 120-mile walk over 10 days. By nightfall, he had simply made up his mind: he was going to do it, whatever it took. And he did. He kept up just fine with the foot race, and he had the second-best time of his life. The first being car racing, of course.

It was with that same can-do competitive spirit, a couple of years later, that he decided to learn to fly an airplane. He wanted to know how to land just in case I had a "bad hair day."

Petra: "Ladies, start your engines."

Don't Lose Your Head

Your neck is stronger than you think.

The human head weighs, on average, about 11 pounds.

With a helmet on, it comes in at around 14 pounds.

All that poundage is perched on a slender muscular stalk called your neck.

Braking, acceleration, and cornering in a race car can easily impose a force of 2G or more on the old noggin. So, under those conditions, it feels like 28 pounds—75% more than the heaviest bowling ball.

During an endurance race a car might traverse, say, 800 laps and 6,400 corners, repeatedly subjecting drivers' necks to many thousands of massive back-and-forth and side-to-side G loads.

Neck and shoulder fatigue become a real factor.

It behooves a driver to make muscle toning a part of their preparation.

Or he/she will surely have a pain in the neck.

That's a good reason, as two pilots in the cockpit are handier than one. But I wondered if he would come to outpilot me and start advising that I needed "more right-rudder" or fewer flaps. For sure, I was grateful he had taught me rudimentary car-racing techniques and that he'd taken the lead to compete in racing a recreational sailboat. My learning to fly certainly benefited from these experiences. But strangely, I wanted flying to be my own show.

So, when I was well into flying lessons on my way to a single-engine private pilot's license, Larry began taking "landing lessons" from my instructor. *Well, here we go*, I thought. *He'll soon know more than I do*. Surprisingly, to both of us, he did not have a natural talent for it. He tried and tried but couldn't land the plane without bumping hard on the runway.

This is where I really began to comprehend competitiveness. Flying is a bit like racing a boat, only faster; racing a boat is a bit like racing a car, only slower. All three sports require a situational hyper-awareness vis-a-vis time and speed. All three require concentration, anticipation, keeping calm and sometimes out-planning others. I found that I was good at these, and my flying skills were built on them. I had acquired some of these skills from Larry.

So even though he did learn the basics of flying and could have (possibly?) landed a plane in an emergency—probably knocking the landing gear off in the process—it was not Larry's "thing." I was secretly gleeful about this revelation (a bit *competitive*?) because— *ta-dah*—I'd finally found a sport I was better at. It made me a little smug. Anyway, I decided it was for the best because if he had embraced flying, Larry would have started airplane racing immediately.

PART **4** — WINNING, THE ONLY OPTION

Chapter 18: **Neenah**

"NO CAMERAS • NO TOURS"

MPI FRONT-DOOR SIGN

A phone call, out of the blue:

"Hello, I'd like to speak to Larry Perkins."

"This is Larry."

"Hi, Larry, we've never met, but I have your old car, your GTO, chassis number 3223 GT. We're planning to restore it completely and win some more trophies with it."

Whaaaat?! Totally stunned ... Larry struggled for a cogent reply ....

"Well, that sounds fantastic. I've wondered for years where the old buggy was. Or even if she still existed. Last I heard, she was headed for the Far East."

"She's back now, but she needs work. There's almost no documentation, lots of racing mods were done and most of the people who did them are gone."

"Yeah, I know. Some were my old buddies. I miss those clever guys."

"Well, I'm glad you're still around; we think you could be a walking encyclopedia on this car. My organization is starting a full-scale restoration, and we'd like your help to get it right."

"Jeez, that's amazing ... like a real ghost from the past! What would you have me do?"

"Just share your personal knowledge with the project. I'll put you in touch with Wayne Obry, one of the best restorers there is. He's starting on the car now, and you guys can take it from there."

And so, after this wake-up call from the Scuderia di Bari organization, Larry's life took another turn in the road. Of course, he couldn't resist the offer. His assignment was very loosely defined: remember details, especially mods and irregularities for which

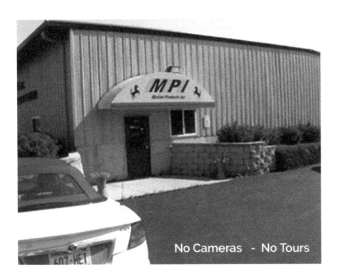

No Cameras - No Tours

no documentation ever existed. Do whatever he could to help make the car—sexy old Sophia—unbeatable in the eyes of absolutely the most knowing and demanding concourse judges in the world. Not a state or region or country... but the world!

The Pebble Beach Concours d'Elégance ("a contest of elegance") is a charitable event held each year on the Pebble Beach Golf Links near Carmel, California. As the finale of Monterey Car Week every August, it is open to prewar and postwar collector cars, which are judged for authenticity, function, history and style.

Competition classes are defined by type, marque (manufacturer), coachbuilder, country of origin and time period. Expert judges select first-to-third-place finishers for each class and confer a Best of Show on one car among the class winners. Honorary judges—individuals who have made significant contributions to the automotive industry or motorsports—award trophies recognizing standout vehicles as well as memorial awards to honor noted automotive industry persons. More than 10,000 spectators attend this spectacular event to admire some of the most important and beautiful vehicles in existence.

Pebble Beach is considered the most prestigious contest of its kind, and Larry was joining a team whose modest target was to win the 2011 Pebble Beach Concours d'Elégance 50th Anniversary Tribute to the Ferrari GTO. It would be the rough equivalent, in the classic car community, of scaling Mount Everest.

On a nice spring day in 2011, Larry flew from Denver to Appleton, Wisconsin, and early the next morning found the Motion Products Inc. location in the nearby town of Neenah. He was severely underwhelmed. "*World-class* is definitely not the right label," he thought, "Something more like, 'Oh-no, another tin-sided car shop.'"

As Larry approached the entrance, a single door on a corner of the windowless sheet-metal building, he was struck by the unpretentious industrial surroundings ... and a stern warning sign: **NO CAMERAS · NO TOURS**. Hmmm. Was this an alert that secrets really did lie within?

Once inside the faceless building, he was in for a dramatic surprise. MPI is one of the premier vintage car restoration facilities in … yes … the world. If you owned a collector's-only irreplaceable specimen of automotive preeminence—and you were inclined to commission the project—Wayne Obry and his extraordinary crew could transform your gem into a priceless, absolutely correct, prize-winning marvel. Chances are, it'd be pretty good for a trip to town too.

Another important feature of MPI's operating model is total confidentiality. Many owners of collector cars prefer not to have their status or whereabouts discussed publicly, and with Motion Products they are assured that their business will be conducted with complete discretion. Thus, the No Cameras sign on the door.

The MPI entrance let into a big open office fairly crammed with small desks and people already busy with the day's work. Larry introduced himself to a friendly lady named Debbie who said, "Wayne will be in any minute, and he'll get you some coffee." (*So, the Big Kahuna comes in late, and* he *fetches the coffee?)*

Larry parked himself on a well-used couch against the wall and inspected a showcase filled, unmethodically, with trophies, medals, nostalgic photos, car models and other auto bric-a-brac. An adjacent glass-walled showroom held a small herd of vintage cars resting their aged but fresh-looking bones.

Within minutes, sure enough Wayne greeted him. He stood well over six feet, and was middle-aged, slim of build, graying at the temples, with a quick smile. No promoter's swagger or props (though he did have a pipe, ready at hand and almost never lighted).

It seemed the two men offered mutually pleasant surprises to one another. It was their first meeting, and neither had any real idea what to expect. The GTO owner had given Larry no background on the MPI operation. Since no one then associated with the car had ever met Larry, Wayne had been given no hints either.

Larry had visualized an entrepreneur, maybe with a big cigar and a corner office overlooking a sea of expensive metal. Wayne in turn would have been justified in imagining a grizzled old codger with an insecure grasp of things automotive and a fading memory of the "old days." Fortunately, they would have both been wrong. In 10 seconds flat they became friends.

A private corner office? None. Wayne sat at a small desk in the middle of the big busy room. Soon Wayne introduced Larry to his technical assistant, Dustin, the receptionist/

office administrator, Debbie, and MPI partner, Bill. Then they set out through a back hall-way into the main shop in search of the coffee pot.

"So, how was your trip from Denver? Gettin' hot down there yet?"

"Oh, tolerable … Colorado's still fine, but not nice and cool like here."

"This is a great area. 'Course we're used to the cold. Don't start puttin' on sweaters 'til it gets down to about 20 … below, that is." Huge grin.

"Now, remind me how you got tangled up in this project anyhow."

"Well, the GTO's owners have been following the historical trail, and it led them to me. It turned out I can remember stuff about the car and the races that isn't documented anywhere. So, they sent me to you."

"Terrific … welcome aboard. We'll sure try to squeeze all that truth out of you we can, and it'll really help us in getting things right. As you'll see this week, we're all about strict authenticity."

And then Wayne escorted Larry through another door into his wizard's realm.

One's first visit to a top-of-the-line restoration shop is stunning. All the senses are triggered. Exotic cars and their intriguing fragments, of every color, shape, and size, are scattered about, seemingly at random, on scrupulously clean surfaces under bright lights. Oil and paint and hot welding odors permeate the air. Mechanics and artisans transform metal, and upholsterers clatter away with their sewing machines on exotic fabrics and custom-tanned hides. The silky finish and heft of a mere door handle conveys the care that goes into handcrafting these vintage automotive artworks.

And the acid bite of less-than-totally-fresh coffee from a pot in the corner completes the sensory assault. This is Car-Guy Heaven.

Bang, bam, squeak, pow, rap-a-tap, buzz, groan, whir, tink, dddddddduh, scritch, zzzzzzzzt, thump. Wayne's place was alive with creative clatter. Magic was happening there … *SHAZAM*!

Every cranny of the big shop was crammed with auto exotica. The space was littered with notable cars—along with their body panels, running gear and accessories. They were in every stage of so-called "frame-off restoration," an arcane, ultra-expensive enterprise that is not for the faint-hearted.

In one workspace, Larry spotted a genuine Old-World craftsman making a brand-new fender for an early '50s Maserati limited-production sports car. His technique and tools were traditional. Working the aluminum by hand and eye, he coaxed it into shape with special hammers over a wooden buck just as the original panel-beater had done 60 years before.

In another corner, a technician was fabricating a radiator for a 1953 Ferrari Cabriolet originally built for the King of Belgium. It was early in the process, and Larry would have the pleasure of watching him complete this marvel in sheet brass as the days went by. On his last day there, they would install the new "old" radiator in the car, connect coolant lines and start the engine. Cool as a cucumber. Not a single leak anywhere!

These methods aren't used for nostalgia or some idea of *purity*—there just aren't any better ways to achieve perfection. In this renovation studio, the past is truly prologue. Larry hadn't even seen his GTO yet, and he was already spellbound.

What is a car exactly? It's a form of transportation; also, the sum of its designer's concepts; selected mechanical components engineered to do a job with decent reliability and perhaps some enhanced capabilities. But every car is really just a well-organized pile of parts.

Certain cars achieve a cachet and become collectible for various reasons. One example may be beautiful, or capable of fantastic performance, or vanishingly rare, or just an unusual (even goofy) design. All cars age, some better than others, so collectible cars usually undergo major restoration by specialists to return them to glory. Collectors often refer to themselves as "custodians." The collection/exhibition game is such that most of these cars undergo multiple restorations.

Cars are part of modern history, and some would say modern art. They have been around for fewer than 135 years, and a working model of the very first one—a Benz—still exists. Most cars are made of tough stuff, anticipating prolonged use. So, with reasonable care, the attainable lifetime of any collector car is thus far unknown.

In a frame-off restoration, a car is completely disassembled, literally reduced to a stack of working components. Everything is labeled, inspected, refurbished, or replaced with like pieces, and checked for authenticity. In a pinch, an irreplaceable part may be fabricated, exactly reproducing the original. Then the whole car is reassembled according to the proper specifications, and—*voila*—a perfect replica is born.

Except that "replica" is a dirty word in the restoration business. Replicas can be very sexy and desirable, but they are not originals. They're copies without provenance and therefore always have lower value than the real thing.

For a car to be genuinely restored, to be *correct*, it must have existed in the first place, created at a certain time, in a factory of origin, with a set of build sheets and an assigned serial number. A significant collectible car becomes known to experts, and its complete history documented. The restorer's normal mission is to return that car to its original factory condition, in a certified fashion.

With the 1962 Ferrari 250 GTO, s/n 3223 GT, the mission was a bit different. The car was the first of its breed and a competition GT car of then unparalleled performance. Its value would always derive from its racing portfolio. Restoring it to its state as it emerged new from the Maranello factory would be meaningless; s/n 3223 GT was not a road car and was never used as such. It was optimized for driving at triple-digit speeds essentially all the time. Modifications began from the first time it turned a wheel.

In a unique and daunting approach to *concours* competition, Wayne Obry's charge was to restore the GTO to its exact configuration at 10:00 a.m. on February 5, 1966, at the start of the inaugural Daytona 24 Hour International Manufacturers Championship. It had finished 19th overall and won 1st in Class Sports 3000. Since Larry had owned and driven the GTO in that race, and since he liked challenges, he was thrilled to be allowed a small part in the upcoming transformation.

Back to the shop tour. As Wayne and Larry moved along, through what seemed like acres of lavish automotive rehab, Sophia was nowhere in evidence. But then they entered another room and there, lurking in its own corner, was the familiar, faintly sinister silhouette of an ancient race car—the ghost of a GTO. *My gosh,* Larry thought, *here's this creepy form, 20 feet away across the shop. Once my love; now a specter.*

A gaunt skeleton, an empty shadowed husk sat, inert, on jack-stands. Where headlights belonged, staring eye sockets. Her air intake, a toothless maw. For this restoration, the GTO's intact body shell stayed attached to its space-frame, but everything else had been removed: engine, wheels, brakes and axles, light fixtures, doors, hood, trunk lid, chrome trim, glass, steering wheel and the entire interior. Its paint had been stripped to bare aluminum. Metal blemishes had been patched and ground smooth. Then the whole thing had been sprayed, inside and out, with a dark shroud of primer.

Not a pretty sight. It looked eviscerated ... lifeless? But Larry knew that Sophia's ultimate destiny was a return to elegance. The sleek sexy form was faintly discernible. She somehow seemed ready to spring like some big dusky predator, lightning quick across the shop, out the door and ... gone.

Wayne and Larry looked her over and noted other owners' changes made through the years. They considered the non-standard mods that would be applied for the restoration, including holes to be cut and metal added. Period racing photos would support genuine and correct details when judging time came. So far, Larry's reunion with this old friend wasn't turning out quite as expected. He just had to ask.

"Wayne, where the hell's the rest of my car?"

But Wayne was waiting with his quick grin and a fresh surprise.

"Let's go look at it," he said, crossing to another section of the shop.

There on massive shelves, in rows of neatly labeled bins and cardboard boxes, was the Ferrari. Every bolt, nut, washer, clip, tubing and wire, down to the axles, ZF gearbox and rear-end, stacked in tiers like cord wood up to the 14-foot-high ceiling. *This* was his old race car. Just a big-ass pile of parts!

As it turned out, the prime mover—the engine—was in yet another part of the shop, having undergone a rebuild and dyno testing. It was ready to be dropped in when final assembly began. They chatted with the mechanic, admiring the Testa Rossa hallmark

components: an awesome array of six Weber dual carbs, twin distributors, familiar Ferrari cam covers, 12 exhaust manifolds snaking out from the heads, the dark bulk of the block and the shallow dry sump.

One could sense the compact menace of the thing. In its heyday, this metal marvel would willingly churn out 300 horsepower at 8,000 rpm, all day and night, for as long as one demanded it. When Enzo said, "Aerodynamics are for people who can't build engines," he meant this Colombo V-12 engineering miracle.

The whole experience was a bit unnerving and reminded Larry of the old saw: *Once you open a can of worms, you can never get all the worms back in the can.* He reflected that it was now May, and the Pebble Beach show was just over the horizon in mid-August.

"I can't believe it, Wayne. I mean, how will you pull all this together practically overnight?"

"Trust me, we do it all the time. But we're still gonna need your help to get it right."

That assertion made Larry feel like a genuine team member as they started down the list of unique race-bred items he was contributing to:

- Front clip—bodywork treatment
- Passenger seat/odd battery box
- Rear window—unusual vents
- Instruments and switch wiring
- Front fenders—holes; missing lights
- Driving lamps—unlike units
- Parking lamps—Porsche parts
- Rear spoiler—attachment method
- Rear wheel-wells—bodywork
- "SNAP" exhaust extractors
- Safety features—essentially none
- Wheels, tires, and spare
- Race numbers and sponsor decals
- Daytona tech inspection decal

Ah, those sponsor decals: Larry had already been researching them before coming to Neenah. Vintage decal replicas were available online, but they were the wrong size, the wrong color or just plain wrong; none were acceptable. Proper ones would need to be created from scratch, using the car's racing photos for patterns and scale.

With the help of Photoshop on the computer and the Fat City decal shop in Appleton, Larry got superior results. The car was shown with precisely correct period stickers for Champion spark plugs, Firebird gasoline, Goodyear tires, Prestolite electrics, competition class markings and the Daytona Speedway scrutineering decal. Black "30" race numbers, with their white background roundels, were to scale; a couple were mounted slightly askew exactly as seen in the period photos.

They settled into a sort of drill. Wayne introduced Larry to the expert MPI crew, who filled him in on their pieces of the puzzle: Bill ran the business office; John made seats and interior upholstery; a master mechanic built the engine; Dustin and Ray hung doors and assembled running gear; a sheet-metal specialist did bodywork; an electrician built and installed wiring harness; various groups worried about livery (paint patterns) and trim.

Wayne reserved the test driving for himself. He and his wife, Debbie, lived on the Wolf River near the charming village of Fremont, so the trip from Neenah to their home

Source of a tiny extra boost

provided a perfect 25-mile shake-down run. Larry could only wonder what the local folks thought of all those exotic cars strutting through their bucolic neighborhood.

Larry stayed out of the way until called on to comment on any aspect he had unique knowledge of, or to search the internet for something crucial. For instance, SNAPs.

The SNAP is a distinctive feature of the Ferrari 250 GTO exhaust system. A barrel with longitudinal slots and spiraled internal vanes, it's attached to the exhaust pipe, extending beyond the lower bodywork. It extracts exhaust gases; reduces back pressure; and adds a final, tiny boost to the total horsepower at high speeds. An extra benefit is to prevent exhaust, which could be drawn into the cockpit, from accumulating around the body's Kamm tail.

For this restoration, MPI had ordered four SNAP's from a special Italian supplier; they came wrapped in tired-looking tissue paper in dog-eared original boxes. They were perfect except that the forward one-third of each was not chrome-plated. Uh-oh, were these authentic? Or were they aftermarket knockoffs?

Noted advisers were contacted, but no one was sure on this one. Larry enlarged and studied old racing photos, checking the actual SNAPs in-period appearance. And the answer was ... the front sections were matte-finished, not chrome plated. Here was a rare quartet of the real thing that had doubtless been sitting on a shelf in Italy for decades! It seemed like a small item, but big *concours* wins are clinched with such niceties.

The days rushed by. Larry worked with a cool local decal designer. He consulted with Wayne and the MPI technicians as, bit by bit, the GTO came together. He spent hours on the phone and the internet. He was in his element again—the car world—after a very long spell in the wilderness.

It was not all cappuccinos and biscottis though. They argued sharply about some remembered details that clashed with the marque gurus' specifications. For example:

- Larry believed the tail spoiler was attached with pop-rivets; the experts insisted it was bolted; the experts won.
- Larry remembered the passenger footwell being blocked by an aluminum panel used at the factory to mount electrical test equipment; Wayne's superior experience indicated that too much weird authenticity could lose the competition. Wayne won.
- Larry remembered the exact circumstances—a crash repair—that resulted in odd little holes in the front fenders, where running lights once were. The holes show in the old

photos. He "won," and the restored car got them. (But the unused wiring was left in place, just the same. In this game, no tiny detail was left to chance.)

Lest anyone question all this obsessive effort, consider the Pebble Beach Concours scoring procedure: a car starts with 100 points, and points are deducted for each fault. The judges routinely assess fine details and measure features to the millimeter. At this competition level, a final score of less than 96 is unacceptable. Losing just four points will take you out of the running.

At last Ferrari 250 GTO s/n 3223 GT emerged from Wayne's wonderland in time to be loaded into the transporter and sent on its way to the most prestigious show in North America. It was euphoric for Larry to have had a small part with such an accomplished team, one that absolutely knew their business—winning *concours d'élégances* and gratifying their customers. Proof positive: This team had a hallway full of victory photos and a shop full of tangible, over-the-top examples.

This crew wasn't experienced at preparing for an endurance race, but Larry came away with complete confidence they could do it if required. In fact, one evening someone asked about that.

"Hey, Larry, do you think the GTO would be good to start a race at Daytona?"

"You're damned right!" he said, "We can go in the morning!" And he meant it.

3223 en route to Pebble Beach

Chapter 19: **The Car Reborn**

My sun sets to rise again.

—ROBERT BROWNING, POET

Benz 1st car - just needs a spoiler

Monterey Car Week delivers a sensory explosion. For car enthusiasts— often labeled "car guys" (or, less kindly, "car nuts")—this extravaganza offers a solid week crammed with everything one could wish for: Trophy-rich design competitions • exotic machinery in motion and at rest • high-end auctions • art shows • historic racing on the famously challenging Laguna Seca track. The crown jewels are "The Quail, a Motorsports Gathering," often called simply The Quail, and the Pebble Beach Concours d'Elégance, where the automotive (and social) crème de la crème is on parade.

If Monterey is an automotive festival, Pebble Beach is its central carnival. On a weekend every August, the celebrated golf club's eighteenth fairway is graced with a cavalcade of automotive distinction; the aggregate value of these treasures is probably incalculable. The makers' names ring down through history, literally dating back to 1886, Carl Benz, and the very first car:

Abarth, AC, Alfa Romeo, Aston Martin, Auburn, Bentley, BMW, Bugatti, Buick, Cadillac, Chevrolet, Chrysler, Cisitalia, Citroen, Cord, Daimler, Deutsch Bonnet, Duesenberg, Facel Vega, Ferrari, Fiat, Ford, Franklin, Ghia, Hispano-Suiza, Hupmobile, Iso Rivolta, Jaguar, Lamborghini, Lancia, Lister, Lotus, Maserati, Maxwell, Mercedes Benz, Packard, Panhard, Pininfarina, Porsche, Renault, Riley, Rolls Royce, Scaglietti, Stutz, Talbot, Triumph, Viper, Zagato … the list seems endless.

Many of the cars participate in two Pebble events. First, on Thursday, is the Tour d'Elégance, a sixty-mile morning drive around the Monterey Peninsula; over a familiar photographers' backdrop, the picturesque Bixby Creek Bridge; and along the Big Sur Coast. This year's tour is being led by the famed 1955 Mille Miglia-winning Mercedes 300 SLR, race number 722, driven then and today by Sir Stirling Moss. Second in line is Ferrari 250 GTO 3223 GT, race number 30, with noted Ferrari expert David Seilestad at the wheel and Alan Boe, Ferrari judge, historian, writer and passenger, hanging on for dear life.

The high point is a lunchtime stop in Carmel-by-the-Sea, the rare cars being parked in rows on Ocean Avenue, allowing admirers to schmooze with owner/drivers and salivate over these gems. The tour stop is a bargain; it presents these consummate machines to fans, up close, in the open, admission free.

On Sunday, the Pebble Beach Concours d'Elégance presents the week's climax. The staid lodge presides over a setting as specialized as it is breathtaking. The immaculate lawn sports celebratory flags, white crowd-control chains, vendor tents along one side, and more than 250 of the most prized cars in the world. Food and drink are sampled all around. The pageant plays out against a spectacular backdrop of Carmel Bay stretching out to sea.

An affluent-looking crowd further spices up the scene. The men (except for the judges) dress casually. Many ladies prefer to sashay a bit, though, adorned with big, showy hats; elaborate frocks; and plenty of shiny baubles. Some of them are "car guys" too.

Sunday is the Really Big Day. Avid fans begin arriving early, in a tradition they call "Dawn Patrol," turning out in misty morning light to admire and photograph the cars assembling on the field of battle.

Custom transporters, parked at the Equestrian Center a half-mile uphill behind the clubhouse, have brought the lion's share of competitors to Pebble. Last-minute preparations have been done without gawkers underfoot. Long rows of vans, many equipped with lifts and workshops, have discharged a glittering array of automotive stars. The cars, of every size and color, will be polished to a spotless sheen meant to make spectators blink in the seaside glare. Their engines hum, grumble, sputter, crackle. The aromas of fuel and exotic oils meld with the perfume of freshly mown polo field turf.

Crews drive the cars down from the Equestrian Center to the "Grass," taking longer than you would think. Even with stewards directing traffic, a jam ensues. Race cars like the

Pebble Beach Tour d'Elegance
presented

START

PROVA
GTO

David Seielstad with friend Sophia

On the grass - Pebble Beach Concours d'Elégance

Sophia and her siblings

GTO, with no cooling fans, tend to overheat. For them the drill is ... join the queue ... shut the engine off ... wait for a gap to open ... restart ... creep forward to close the gap ... stop and shut off ... wait ... repeat.

Once on the fairway, cars are driven to their assigned positions. With more than 200 vehicles to be arranged, Pebble staff members have streamlined the process through the years. Occasionally, there is some inadvertent wheel-spinning and disapproving frowns all around—this is a golf course after all. But ultimately, the fairway is studded with rows of show cars and things settle down for a long day of praise and approval, lots of "*oohing* and *aaahing,*" schmoozing, selfie-snapping and surreptitious touching (of cars, mostly) by an appreciative crowd.

The 2011 *Concours* includes a unique lineup. Twenty-one of the existing 36 Ferrari 250 GTOs, plus the original prototype (250 GT Sperimentale, s/n 2643), are arrayed in one long cordon, like a stationary royal motorcade along the waterfront. It's nearly inconceivable: sixty percent of the most prized cars on Earth, worth perhaps a billion and a half dollars, perch on a patch of grass you could cover with a circus tent.

On this green starting grid, the GTOs crouch like big rapacious felines, spring-loaded to pounce and devour some high-velocity mechanical rabbit. At first glance they appear

Every detail, no matter how elusive, is judged

Judging Elegance - Andrea Zagato, Denise McCluggage, Jochen Mass, John Surtees

as sleekly identical industrial forms, but a closer look reveals that each is subtly unique. They're tarted up in a rainbow of racing liveries—red, green, silver, blue, white, striped and trimmed—all breathtaking. Many flaunt big race numbers on their noses and flanks, leaving no doubt that these are not grocery-getters. Unleashed on the racetrack, as several were at Laguna Seca yesterday, they're happy to demonstrate to the youngsters there's still plenty of hustle left in these gorgeous old girls.

It's still early when the judges begin to appear, gathering at the first of their assigned cars. They are easily identified by their "uniforms"—dark blue blazers, light trousers, white shirts and ties, iconic straw fedoras—and they carry the tools of their trade … clipboards with the particulars of each car in competition.

This team of judges is key to Pebble Beach's influence. They comprise a handpicked body of renowned experts on the marques at hand, and their evaluations are mind-bendingly detailed and meticulous. They have personally owned, raced, wrenched on, judged and studied the history of the cars they assess. They are, in many cases, the globally recognized authorities, and their word is law in this contest of excellence and correctness. Their august presence, as they approach each car and its crew, is amiable but intimidating.

For this 2011 event, Larry has joined the support team for The Car. He is on hand to answer questions about undocumented racing modifications that may not be familiar to the judges. For a touch of authenticity, the team has outfitted him in a vintage ensemble,

MPI Dream Team - Debbie Obry, Wayne Obry, Ryan Vandenberg, Ray Ruggerre

complete with a cotton driver's suit, net-back gloves, and an open-face Bell Shorty helmet (all of which would horrify any modern racing-safety advocate). Like any driver, he's a walking display ad; his suit flaunts logos for Ferrari, Goodyear, Champion, Hella, Prestolite, SCCA and Shell.

The judging is intensive. Four experts converge on the car and want to know *everything* about it. They:

- Minutely examine the body work, glass, lighting, interior, trunk, engine bay, wheels, brakes
- Take a variety of measurements (with a millimeter scale!)
- Get underneath (blue blazers, white trousers and all) to inspect the undercarriage, exhaust system, suspension, drive train
- Start the engine, listen for a while, watch for leaks and overheating, rev it a few times, check the gauges, sniff the exhaust for gas or oil fumes, rev it some more
- Check the spare, snap-jack, tool kit contents, safety accessories, and tires

Alan Boe and David Seilestad on Pebble Beach Tour

Finally, the judges examine the leather-bound documentation volume that restorer Wayne Obry provides. It holds factory build sheets, specifications, serial number photos, FIA and ACCUS homologation papers, competition records, ownership history. In other words, a collection of information that verifies the air-tight provenance of this particular car—**Ferrari 250 GT Comp/62 berlinetta, chassis number 3223 GT**—and all its correct components.

They grill Larry about the choice of mismatched driving lamps for the Daytona race represented in this restoration. They want to know the origin of several bodywork modifications and the reasoning behind interior changes peculiar to this car. They are especially interested in non-standard changes to some components, such as the battery location. But everyone understands this is a racing car, where frequent modifications are always driven by necessity rather than style.

They accept Larry's answers in a non-committal way, but it's clear they are observing and noting the tiniest details. These judges seem to walk away knowing more about s/n 3223 GT than anyone who has never taken it apart and reassembled it. And they keep what they know entirely to themselves—at least for the present.

At last, the judging is complete and the officials move on to another car. Larry's team experiences an anticlimax, a huge release of pent-up tension. They all know they're in a high-stakes contest, but they can only remain passive for now. Everything that could have been done was completed last night and early this morning. From here on, all they can do is patiently wait for the results.

For Larry, an acutely competitive person, this is a new experience, and the suspense is excruciating. But the wait also affords a chance to enjoy the grandeur of the surrounding show. He takes a few laps around the grounds to see the sights. Being a sculptor, he's anxious to catch the works in the Automotive Fine Arts Society tent. Kumar Galhotra, head of Lincoln Motor Company, has been quoted as saying "AFAS artists represent the pinnacle of taste and quality." Their show, hosted by two dozen or so world-famous car artists, lives up to expectations, presenting some of the finest paintings, drawings, and three-dimensional representations available anywhere.

Larry, a car guy, is also naturally drawn to the astonishing variety of automotive design displayed on the eighteenth fairway. Every car is a jewel in its own right. All are in some regard significant in the evolution of private transportation over the past century. And to a car they appear to have just come out of the factory door.

And there is the crowd, perhaps the most notable ingredient of the whole extravaganza. Without them, the show would be a non-thing. Cruising the stunning green space, Larry finds himself caught in a vortex of car experts, collectors, fans of particular marques, photographers, car crews, well-off older gents, extravagantly dressed younger beauties, TV crews, journalists, runners, waiters, more photographers, the all-important judges, various *Concours* officials and just casual viewers out for a (pricey) day's amusement.

Ferrari owners pause to chat beside s/n 3223 GT, including some who have cars in today's show. A couple are fellow competitors in the stunning array of GTOs. They comment politely to Larry on the appearance of "his" car. Jay Leno, TV personality and prominent car guy, strolls through, admiring the hardware and casually shaking hands. Jay's famously eclectic vehicle collection does not yet include a Ferrari GTO. Nice of him to stop by though.

A TV reporter and a crew lugging bulky camera gear catch sight of Larry in his driver's suit and approach to find out what's going on. They stand near The Car urging Larry to recount a short history of how it and he came to be here. Booms with padded microphones dangle overhead. An intimidating camera lens looms close. Larry looks around for a mirror to check his makeup and makes some brief remarks.

The interviewer seems to struggle with the improbability of this tale; ex-soap salesman and rocket scientist once successfully competed in international endurance racing? In this very car? And is still around to tell about it fifty years later?

Finally, a welcome, familiar face appears—Larry's friend, Denise McCluggage— reporter, writer, race driver and doyenne of the motor sports community for decades. Denise is fitted out with the standard judge's blazer, straw hat (gussied up with pretty flowers) and clipboard. Small and pert, she somehow seems doubly imposing, in full command of her impressive team: Andrea Zagato, head of the venerable company that bears his name; Jochen Mass, seasoned F1 and sports car driver with a Le Mans win to his credit; and John Surtees, winner of five World Championships on motorcycles and F1 cars.

Denise declares, "Our daunting little task, on this field groaning with classic goodies, is to bestow the award for the Most Elegant Sports Car. Wish us luck, Larry."

As the afternoon wears on, a certain stir drifts across the grounds. Award ceremonies will begin soon. There are many classes to be recognized, culminating with the judges'

Wayne, Larry and Marcel ready to pop the cork

More of MPI team - Dustin Wetmore

number one choice, Best of Show. And what a show it is. The winner's stage, a ramped platform in front of the lodge, affords spectators a sustained view of each victor in motion, with its proud driver and passengers giggling and waving in delight.

Since all cars come to Pebble Beach fully operational, every winner will be driven onto the flower-bedecked dais for all to see and applaud. The area will light up like a Hollywood sound stage as a staggering number of photos are snapped. Formal trophy awards will be made by men in spiffy brass-buttoned blue blazers with white chinos, and pretty girls in stylish peach dresses and smart chapeaux. The pomp is intensified by accolades from winners' rivals, enthusiastic fans and esteemed experts. The crowd's enthusiasm is stunning as winning cars are directed down the ramp to a nearby enclosure, giving spectators a second close-up peek at the "Best of the Best." Getting here is not easy, or cheap, and the short trip across that space, with a long pause at the top, is very heady stuff.

Larry's team is hunkered down in beach chairs on the edge of the exhibit space. The waiting has seemed endless, and the suspense is nearly intolerable. They wonder whether they will be included in the next part of the spectacle. "Have we won a spot in the finals?

Do we get a bottle of that bubbly? Which way do we go ... **if** we go?"

Time tick ... tick ... ticks by

Tick ... tick

Then the call comes!

They've made it...they're in the finals!

Their team is in a sudden flurry. Wayne rushes over to Larry. "C'mon, get your hardhat on. We're going!" And they sprint over to the GTO. They jump in, if one can be said to jump into a car with a 47-inch-high roof. Larry cranks the key, starts up, blips the engine a couple of times. They're directed into a line creeping its way through the crowd of spectators. Ahead are two more red GTOs snaking toward the winner's dais. Thus far the cars and the winning order have yet to be announced. Attendants with iridescent vests wave them closer to the lodge and into a staging space.

Slow going

Damn, they're stopped and waiting

Race cars, and racers, hate waiting

PA background chatter and crowd noise grow louder. It's hard to hear inside the cockpit. The GTO enjoys a seminal reputation and an epic following. Many fans have never actually seen—or heard—a Ferrari GTO before. People are keen to check out these old beauties as they rev and strain at the bit. A Ferrari V12 race engine at idle sounds busier than most cars at full steam.

Wayne and Larry wait as patiently as they can. They wave at their personal support team cheering from the sidelines. Petra, friend and former s/n 3223 GT broker David Gizzi, Debbie Obry and the MPI crew, have pushed to the front of the crowd, and the crowd itself is jostling as close to the cars as barrier ropes allow.

Larry fidgets, nervously blips the engine. *RrrrRuffah ... RrrrRuffah.* "Hey Wayne," he teases, "when we go, how about I stretch 'er out a little ... do a couple of nice wheelies here on the lawn?"

Wayne's face turns the color of boiled haddock. "Oh, SHIT, Larry, PUH-LEEEZE don't do that!"

The big overhead-cam mill chatters and whines

Probably thinks it's going somewhere, fast

Water temp creeps up

Shut her off or keep her running?

Aw, let her run, at least to 105° C

Larry and Wayne check out the competition. On their left flank is s/n 3943 GT, wearing a tricolor stripe and race #6, a car with a rich racing history in original and historic events. On the right is s/n 3765 LM, carrying race #7, one of three GTO-type berlinettas built with four-liter engines. In the mid-60s, 3765 LM was retrofitted with a three-liter engine and successfully raced in several events as a 250 GTO. The proud owner, James Jaeger, has now fastidiously restored it to its 1962 "330" configuration.

At last, the PA system blares. The announcements for "Class M-2, Ferrari 250 GTO 50th Anniversary Awards" have begun. An official, reminiscent of a race starter, has positioned himself out front. He's ready to wave the competitors up to the platform in their proper order. All eyes are on him, and time seems suspended. For Larry there's a familiar taut readiness; this is as close to a grid start as he has experienced in many decades. He has to consciously relax his right foot; he says softly to himself, "This is not a race, Larry."

Temp alert, Larry ... 105° C ...

The noise level rises as the PA comes alive with an announcement they can't quite hear. People begin their applause. Wayne and Larry fix their gaze on the "starter," who points to #6 on their left and waves it forward toward the Winner's Ramp. As the third-place car pulls out, Wayne says, "Well, looks like we're next." A long pause ensues and there's a small flurry on the platform, while the 3943 GT driver receives congratulations and his trophy—and Sophia's motor begins to overheat. Larry shuts her off.

They wait some more. Then the PA barks again, the crowd stirs, the "starter" moves into position, Larry starts the engine again, Wayne claps his hands, and they get set to take off for the big moment. But the official points to the car on their right, #7, GTO 3765 LM, and waves it toward the ramp for the second-place prize. What? Oh, Wow!

Larry gives the engine another cooling-off period. But he and Wayne yell and try clapping each other on the shoulder in the confines of the little cockpit. Obviously #30, s/n 3223 GT, dear old Sophia, has won, over 20 of her sisters, in the nonpareil 2011 Pebble Beach Ferrari 250 GTO 50th Anniversary competition.

This is almost better than a race, Larry thinks, and starts the engine. The steward waves them forward, and they climb the winner's ramp to the crowd's acclaim. They open the doors, and judges hand over an engraved silver tray and a magnum of Mumm Napa champagne. A pretty lady proffers a blue ribbon and a colorful bouquet. It's a huge

Ribbons, flowers, silver, a pretty lady ... Wow!

triumph topping off a long, tortuous saga.

Sophia's motor is running. Her temperature gauge creeps up. No one seems to mind very much.

After all the hoopla, the TV crew shows up again in the winner's enclosure. The reporter wants to add a few more tidbits to his tape:

> Sir, did you actually race this car back in the day?
>
> *You bet; even to the grocery store once. I didn't get a ticket.*
>
> Is it your Ferrari?
>
> *Are you kidding? I couldn't afford the dust on this buggy now.*
>
> There were about 10,000 fans cheering you on when you drove up to the Winner's Dais—was that like coming full circle from 1966?
>
> *Well, it's pretty thrilling. I hadn't expected to ever sit in that seat again. It's a real honor to have a guest-drive in this amazing Pebble Beach race.*

GTO 3223 GT ... top of the heap

The trophy tray is lying in front of the car on the manicured fairway.
The inscription reads:

Dom Pérignon
~
61st Pebble Beach Concours d'Elégance
250 GTO Class
1er Prix

Chapter 20: Wives, Wine and Winners

"Mister ELEGANT!!"

—SCUDERIA DI BARI

Carmel, California: I, Petra, run across the fairway of Pebble Beach as fast as my ridiculous high heels can go in dewy grass, hanging onto my oversized, floppy, black and white Italian stylized hat. I am late to see Larry's team get the award (that is, *if* he gets one) for restoring his old Ferrari to its exact 1966 race condition. As of last night, it was touch and go as to whether The Car would even qualify in this Concours d'Elégance competition. There was some possible problem with having the original engine or gearbox, so I have all my fingers crossed. Larry says, "Not to worry." (Not worrying is his style.)

I pass dear friends, Nancy and Jim Stainton, who have driven us here. Nancy strikes the perfect note, with her prize-winning hat, flared skirt—a glamorous vintage-era knockout. She and Jim, hard-core Car Guys, pose in front of a jazzy carriage where they'd tested out the seats.

I run past arrays of the world's most sumptuous automobiles—sleek racers, spectacular sports cars, spiffy sedans—and stop in my tracks, stunned by a French 1949 Delahaye 175 S Saoutchik Roadster, possibly swoopier than any Italian art deco auto ever designed. The sculpted, wing-like, periwinkle-blue slender stacks of fenders that go on forever take my breath away. While I salivate over it, I notice a martini bar and smell a sharp tang of wine and other spirits hanging in the air. I jump in line to grab a pink Cosmopolitan with lime twist, gulp a big sweet/sour swallow so I can run without spilling the martini, and then take off again, trying not to trip over my skirt. I pass a human parade of some of the world's wealthiest, these vintage car owners, in fine feathers, bejeweled silks and

"Car guys" Nancy and Jim Stainton

herringbone jackets. Most everyone is sporting a chapeau, like at the Kentucky Derby, a 30s or 40s classic topper, and I straighten my own super-sized hat, amazed that I've managed to keep it from being crushed all the way from Denver to California.

The brisk breeze off the ocean cools the sweat from my sprint and brings whiffs of wet sand, fresh-tide shells and pungent seaweed. They mingle with the musky aromas of Cuban cigars as I run by the Smoking Tent. I zoom past rows of formidable Ferraris parked on a bias to the sea. They are mostly Chinese red but also a bright chartreuse green and one a taxicab yellow.

I pause to admire a foreboding dark sedan that has drawn a crowd. Someone says, "That's Adolph Hitler's car." Shocked, I peek inside at cracked leather seats where the evil dictator had ridden out WWII in comfort. Even though we are forbidden to touch any cars, I can't help myself and cop a feel with my thumb and as I hurry on. Passing the judges' podium, I see the show's MC, Jay Leno, step up in shiny shoes. Sheryl Crow in flouncy paisley cowgirl attire has just finished strumming and singing to 10,000 listeners, "I've Got a Ticket to Ride."

Larry has been bestowed a ticket to drive—an honor given him by the GTO's proud owners to drive into the Winner's Circle. Finally, I make it to a fence just as he and two other finalists are lined up, waiting to see which team becomes the lucky winner. I stand beside David Gizzi, who had been a long-term custodian of The Car years before while commissioned to sell it to previous owners.

"What was it like, driving it?" I asked David.

"Unbelievable. Fast and fun! Best. Ride. Ever."

I look over at Larry and know his excitement level is skyrocketing.

"Do you think they'll really win?" I say, breathless.

"Of course, they will win," says David, looking at probable stars in my eyes. "It's in the stars."

And before I know what is happening, the third and second place cars are announced, respectively, and move forward, leaving Larry (the winner!) to coax the rough, roaring engine to life and proceed carefully to the Winner's Circle as cheering fans part in his path. There he and passenger Wayne Obry accept a large trophy from a beautiful woman, and I can see Larry's face in the open window. It's reddish and *g-l-o-w-i-n-g*. His aura is lighting up the car, the winner's pad and the whole of Pebble Beach. Perhaps the astronauts on the International Space Station can see the glow from space. As Larry drives away, I'm sure he must be restraining himself from doing some kind of goofy stunt with Sophia.

The excitement is definitely *not* over as the stewards send a call for GTO s/n 3223 GT to return to the winner's stand. The owners, Scuderia di Bari, are to receive another trophy. This time Larry is joined for the ride by Marcel Massini, noted Ferrari historian and technical expert. They take the now more familiar path up to the circle and are again greeted by judges and flower girls. They are showered with congratulations and receive the Most Elegant Sports Car award, a glossy silver abstract car sculpture and yet another nice bottle of champagne. Marcel immediately volunteers to look after the wine and allow no harm to come to it.

After being kissed and warmly hugged by about a hundred people, each refilling my glass, I hike to the reception area where the restoration team has gathered.

Larry is there, striking and handsome in his brilliant racing suit with the original patches and crash helmet. On a sunny grassy knoll, oceanside, he stands roped off from spectators, alone with The Car, which is polished to such a high gloss I can see his sharp reflection in it. It looks like twin Larrys, both holding court, showing off the famed Ferrari. A royal blue ribbon is tied to the windshield wiper, flipping in the wind. I duck under the rope to read it, stumbling on my skirt and spilling my drink. "FIRST PLACE." *Whoo hoo!* And best of all … in front of The Car is a silver tray trophy engraved *61st Pebble Beach Concours d'Elégance 250 GTO Class 1st Prize,* as well as the car statue for the *Strother MacMinn Most Elegant Sports Car.* Larry, beaming his Cheshire Cat grin, is identical to his race photo forty-five years earlier in 1966. The Car's "dream team" has earned not one, but two of the show's top awards. Larry is back in his element of winning: they've won bigtime at the Bigtime. This, dawning in my consciousness, is what it means to come full circle. *This* is coming full circle at its pinnacle.

Hot tears fall from my eyes as I watch him claim victory. I know it will be days before I can sort out all that my senses have taken in this psychedelic afternoon. It seems a genuine

Spectacular surprise!

miracle, the two of us being here with The Car, like accidentally finding ourselves under the arch of a triple rainbow. I think back to the day in 1964 when a teenage girl ran out of that fiery Florida grandstand having watched #82 go around and around. If someone had told her, at 15, that in 2011 she would be here with that car and its driver, together at the greatest car show on Earth—and that she would be a genuine "car girl"—she would have cackled a laugh that stretched from the Atlantic to the Pacific Ocean.

I try but cannot imagine how rock stars or movie stars handle the constant, overwhelming adulation of fans. Larry, The Car Star, is having his micro-taste of it for one single afternoon—his fifteen minutes of fame, as it were. After hours in high heels, after rushing across the golf green snapping photos and delivering food for Larry, I need to sit down and rest my feet. He needs to balance his carbs, I fear, or he might keel over. Actually, I am the one who feels dizzy. He doesn't seem to be flagging at all—despite the previous day's multiple festivities and little sleep. The barrage of noise and sights, excitement and events, have created a surrealistic vibe. Plus, effects of the bubbly. I am like Alice in Wonderland when she drinks the potion to make her shrink. The endless rows of exotic autos, the staggering numbers of aficionados, the non-stop awards—it all keeps getting bigger and bigger.

There is a tiny spot by the ocean for tiny me. I spread out my cape to sit on, dropping my stuff in a heap. Here I can escape, listen to the band's music, and relax, maybe write a poem. Seagulls waddle over, examine my hat, possibly as a potential nest. I swish it at them. *Shoo!* I breathe in the ocean air and think about sailing. We never won a sailing race, but we came close. We might have sailed to Fiji if I hadn't chickened out. I gaze at the bright blue sea, in the direction of Fiji. I glance back at Larry and The Car. He is still going to and fro like the Energizer Bunny ... expounding, demonstrating, posing, gesticulating, so utterly stoked, surrounded by judges, reporters, fans and photographers, TV crews, team members and their tireless wives. I should be standing there by him. This seems to be confirmed by Sheryl Crow who is belting out "Stand by Your Man" ... "and show the *worrrld* you love him ..." *You got that right, Sheryl. Help me get over there!*

But I don't move; it's more fun to watch the parade of beautiful people in their festive outfits and think of the old days. I notice a stylish woman, near The Car. She has on a 1930s chemise of layered lace, diaphanous chiffon, and other frou-frou. I think how it is rather low cut for the 30s. A lavish, opulent chapeau with a tall, coquettish feather. A little younger than I am. There she is again, movie-star smiling at Larry and hanging on his every word. Hundreds of people want to talk with him today. He doesn't need *food*—he is filling up on adoration. I pan the area and see a line has queued, waiting to speak with him. I focus back on Larry—the woman is still there. Now she is playing with her long silver-blonde curls. Now she is tipping up her sunglasses as he chats. Now she is moving in closer to gather him in the shade under her umbrella. *That's it. Enough!* ... I jump up, dumping the glass and throwing my stuff together in a bundle. *Gangway! It's one of those fucking Groupies!* He'd mentioned the aggressive Groupies to me a few times over the years. I hurry over, tumbling in my high heels, hopping as I strap them on, to see if Larry needs anything.

"Yoo, hoo," I call. He doesn't hear. "Oh, Mr. Perrrr-kins!" He is completely under her spell. I sidle close to him, huffing, just as the vintage fan pulls her skirt up one thigh. I cannot believe my eyes though I'd heard the stories of Groupies' shocking brazenness. "... and here's my scar from the knee operation ... I just had it a month ago," she sniffs. I lean over to examine her scar; Larry bends to better examine her leg. "Oh, my, that looks *grotesque*," I say, grabbing his chest, pulling him back. "I shudder to even think about

"It was in the stars"

A serious car guy congratulates Larry

surgery," I say, trembling my head and torso in mock fear.

   She stops in mid-flirt, lowering her designer sunglasses halfway to inspect me like an insect. The Groupie makes an exaggerated show of assessing my hat, fallen askew, then my cleavage and my shoes. I look down. There's gull poop on them.

   "And who ... are *you?*" she asks.

   It's good that I'm wearing shades, too, so she can't see the knife blades.

   "I'm ... I'm ... his wife," I reply. I should have said "mother." The dress drops to her ankle boots as she lets go of the handful of ruffles.

   "Oh." She twirls the parasol like a girl caught stealing. "I guess I should be running along now. I've got sooo many more cars to see."

   Still, she doesn't go. *Security ... call Security? Do they have a jail in Carmel, California? Isn't Clint Eastwood in charge here?*

   I gesture to the growing line of people behind her. "Yes, please try back later. I'm sure we'll still be here," I say, sighing heavily.

Larry winks at me. Someone breaks into the line to shake his hand. It's Jay Leno.

POSTSCRIPT—The winning continued! The Dream Team won additional top awards at the *2012 Cavallino Classic* in Palm Beach, Florida: 250 GTO Cup (Outstanding example of the legendary 250 GTO); Excellence Cup-1 (Outstanding Restoration Quality and Challenge). Ferrari 250 GTO s/n 3223GT is currently held in a private collection.

Full Circle

Chapter 21: Maranello and Michelangelo

Cars may seem alive, connecting with us, reminding us that we are.

—DARIN ROBERGE, AUTHOR

A year passes. Petra reminisces:

In the fiftieth year after The Car was born, Larry and I received an invitation to stay in Florence, Italy, at the home of Michelangelo, the world's greatest sculptor. Well, it wasn't his house, exactly, but 500 years ago his feet trod very close to this apartment near the Arno River. I could feel his presence there, in the marble sculptures and architecture of the primo Renaissance city. Florence was also the first home of Leonardo da Vinci—arguably the best painter, architect, and inventor of all time—who trekked the same cobbled streets as Michelangelo. Even though their years on earth overlapped (da Vinci was older), they weren't exactly buddies. I'd like to think the two geniuses met for tea to resolve their artistic differences, perhaps, on the Ponte Vecchio bridge. Their spirits spoke to me about art ... car art.

We diverted to Maranello, to the Ferrari Classiche shop on Via Abertone Inferiore for a tour, hosted by Marco Arrighi where we and our friends were treated a bit like racing royalty. Larry discovered that Marco had found records of his racing events in a secure historical archive. This seemed amazing to see Larry's race results from Daytona and Sebring, Florida, decades later in Maranello. The sacred workspace held an array of stunning and notable cars in the midst of restoration and certification, many concealed by tight-fitting red fabric dust covers. Others were being worked on—a TdF LWB berlinetta, one of the Series II GTOs, and the silver GTO 4153 GT. The entire shop was brightly lighted and simply immaculate.

I wasn't allowed to take photos in the courtyard. What? Here we were, may never be again, and no cars were being displayed. I stood disappointed in the empty space and was filled with the ghost of Sophia. What's one little photo of nothing? I snapped it when no one was looking. I had to, *mea culpa*. This is where it all began, where The Car became public on February 24, 1962. There was something remarkable about it being 2012, a half century later. I knew I must memorialize this hallowed ground as the courtyard with yellowish buildings now looked almost identical to 1962 photos. I imagined the exquisite Ferraris that had made their artistic debuts, their performance promises, in this very spot.

We went to lunch at Enzo's charming hangout across the street—Ristorante Cavallino. The four of us were seated alone, far in the back, in a vast room, a sea of unoccupied tables. I'd wanted to sit in the front overlooking the charming patio, over a Lambrusco, and observe the Ferrari fellows and fellas—where Enzo had dined with his staff of designer

Lorenzo stands guard

geniuses. And I believe if I'd been able to speak Italian a bit better, along with some hand language signs, I could have pleaded my case for a spot in the main room by explaining that Larry was royal … a race driver!

Covering every wall were items of Scuderia Ferrari memorabilia, model cars, photographs of Enzo/the cars/drivers/events, paintings, flags, famed wine bottles that lined the ceiling, a blaze of trophies, all set off by the whitest fabric-covered chairs, tablecloths and drapes. Everything in Italy, from the most mundane, serviceable objects to the towering architecture, seemed to be lovingly created and arranged as works of unforgettable art.

Another highlight was a personal tour of Museo Ferrari by director Christos Vahlos. He walked us through each breathtaking room as we learned bits on every car, some of the rarest in the world. It was as though we were marching through time, witnessing the stages of evolution of design and technology. The cars of every F1 champion were displayed along with video, helmets, and other artifacts. One section was devoted to GT cars that Ferrari had fielded over the years. Personally, I was tingling with vibration and awe at seeing all this nostalgia in one building, but it was the artistry—the *car*-tistry—that really got to me. These cars were designed by people with passion in their souls. As far as my favorite, I wanted to take home the so-called "Bread Van," as there was something stylish-though-utilitarian about it. How cool would it be to drive this art piece to pick up teenagers at school!

Back in Florence, Larry was in heaven among master artists as we visited Michelangelo's *David* in the Galleria dell'Accademia. Larry cried when he stood gazing up at this astonishing monument. He knew what Herculean effort and innate talent it had required. His own work was done from clay to wax to bronze, but he admired anyone who could chisel perfection out of stone without the backup of being able to start over in case of a mistake. The incomparable brilliance of the Italian Renaissance sculptors was simply unfathomable. Funny, though, it is believed that Leonardo da Vinci, a rival of Michelangelo, thought far less of sculpture, put less value on sculpture than on paintings. Perhaps that's why Michelangelo did not much like him, allegedly.

I imagined a conversation between Michelangelo and Leonardo when da Vinci developed his car sculpture (which is thought to be the first car design ever).

Mike: Yo, I hear you *finally* created a sculpture?

Leo: Yeah, man, I guess I did. They call it a car wagon.

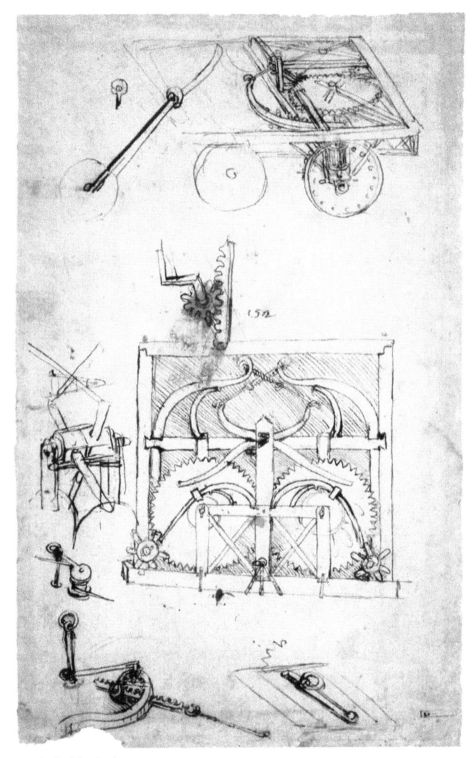

1478 - Da Vinci's dream car

Mike: You mean it moves, like a kinetic sculpture.

Leo: That's the idea. It will travel practically on its own, wherever you want it to go.

Mike: But, dude, it's ugly as sin. Can't you make it look more, like, *aesthetic*?

Leo: It's practical, Mikey. And it can go fast. Watch this … (Leo sets his new car in motion).

Mike: Okay, that's a start. But I think it should be easier on the eyes. Make it beautiful, graceful, with form and lines, dimension and swoop, so that people all over the empire will be stunned into wanting one of their own.

Leo: Are you saying they would want a car wagon if it was *pretty?*

Mike: No, no, 'Nardo! *Sex-y*, not pretty. (Mona's pretty, not sexy. Get it?) Listen, Bub, you make a hot-looking wagon that goes like lightning and even the Pope will bless you.

Leo: (chortling) IT WILL NEVAH HAPPEN!

Yet it did happen, sort of. Consider the Ford GT40 MkIIs. They have a certain utilitarian and even sinister aspect, businesslike and brawny, not particularly *da Vincian*, originally designed with the help of a Dearborn wind tunnel and an IBM computer. There is no mistaking their mission. The Ford MkII was the most powerful, the fastest "car wagon" around, and won a World Championship. Beast vs. beauty. Can we question success?

Well, yes. Italian cars have often dominated in competition too, but somehow the emphasis seems different, more consciously poised and romantic. GTOs, as quintessence of automotive sculpture—as symbiotic masterpieces of form combined with performance— have starred in many art shows. For example, Ralph Lauren has shown Ferraris, including his 250 GTO (s/n 3987 GT), in the Musée du Louvre. And Ferrari s/n 3223 GT became officially and universally "elegant" when winning the Most Elegant Sports Car trophy at the 2011 Pebble Beach Concours d'Elégance, followed by top restoration awards at the 2012 Cavallino Classic. And nothing on wheels has yet surpassed the utterly voluptuous sensuality of the Ferrari 330 P3/4. It's safe to say that Italian examples of *art objects you can drive* will endure long after their status as mere mechanical marvels has waned.

Chapter 22: Invulnerable?

"If a single one of you ... think for a second what we do is safe, you're hugely mistaken. All these drivers put their life on the line ... and people need to appreciate that ...."

LEWIS HAMILTON, 2019, 6-TIME WORLD CHAMPION

CRASH. In racing, it's a catch-all word: shorthand for a 5-mph bump on the grid, a 100-mph car-to-car wallop on the track, an ass-over-tea-kettle-roll-'er-up-in-a-ball cruncher and everything in between. Stock car racing folks say "wreck;" Brits prefer "shunt." Anyhow it's all the same thing ... a hot mess.

- Crashes happen. Drivers and cars are not created equal. Equipment, skills, and judgment can all fail, offering proof of Newton's Laws of Motion. In the right (bad) circumstances, a 2,500-pound car can soar like a bird. Fortunately, most crashes are minor, damaging hardware and egos but not flesh and bone. Modern safety measures help keep the carnage to a minimum. But it wasn't always so. The Lewis Hamilton quote above applied at least as well in the early 1960s, when Larry entered the sport, as it does today.

- It was a time when, according to another safety-conscious World Champion, Jackie Stewart, "Motor racing was dangerous, and sex was safe." There weren't many trackside barriers; circuits were marked off with flimsy hay bales and little peach baskets; pit lanes were separated from main straights by painted white lines on the pavement. Cars plunged off the road into other cars, light poles, fences, walls, barns, grass, gravel, cliffs, forests—calamities facetiously called "agricultural racing."

- Some cars had rudimentary rollover bars; some had none. Seatbelts were more or less optional, and there were no five-point harnesses. Closed-car drivers frequently wore no goggles. Gloves weren't required, shoes of any sort were OK and many drivers wore nylon socks—a grim mistake in even a minor blaze. Onboard fire extinguishers were rare; fuel cells non-existent. Nomex fire-retardant clothing wasn't widely adopted until about 1967. Until then, drivers' suits were cotton, dipped in boric acid solution, offering a few seconds' protection in a gasoline fire ... and of course all the sports cars ran on gasoline.

Headgear offered little more protection than polo helmets. Some *were* polo helmets! The latest Snell-approved models were open-faced shells with polystyrene foam padding inside. Like many drivers, Larry preferred the comfortable "shorty" style that covered one's ears and neck with nice soft (easily torn) leather. Goggles were a mix of aviator and motorcyclist styles; some were OK, some nearly useless. One rule was strictly enforced though: no contact lenses. One might pop out and turn a driver into a blinking, squinting Cyclops. A Porsche driver, Bill Benker, once reported driving an entire 40-lap race with one lost lens glinting brightly from the bottom of his right goggle frame. Given all these hazards, why would any normally cautious person climb into a car and go racing? Did they, or their fans, or anyone else think they were invulnerable? The short answer is "No." People drawn to racing were cautious, just not quite in the usual way. Like other competitive athletes, they focused on personal performance and took whatever precautions were available at the time.

- It never seemed that spectators really wished to see race drivers hurt. But a high level of risk always made racing a big draw. It was part of the challenge, part of why drivers were admired, a bit like astronauts venturing into space. They did things that were out of the ordinary—things that produced an adrenalin rush like no other and, along with it, they put on a good show. Drivers appreciated the danger. They realized they were not invincible. But they didn't brood about it.

- In Larry's early days he seldom saw anyone get genuinely HURT. Something would occasionally go wrong. A driver would get sideways and roll his car ... *whump ... whump* and walk away. Or someone would get too eager and whack someone else, with a metallic *clunk* followed by a lot of arm-waving and loud cussing. There was a medical tent and a doctor or two in attendance, and an ambulance would sometimes be called onto the track. Motor racing didn't really look all that perilous.

- Larry really liked the drivers' on-track style too. They appeared to be in one of just three states: accelerating furiously, going like hell, or braking abruptly—amid big doses of tire-spin and see-sawing of steering wheels and clouds of dust. Yet they seemed basically composed, like they were out for a Sunday drive. He witnessed a lot of people performing allegedly reasonable feats with cars ... at over 140 mph.

- After the races there was always plenty of relaxation and camaraderie. Guys stood around guzzling beers, gesturing like fighter pilots bragging about their heroic moves. Lots of vivacious girls seemed irresistibly drawn into the scene, even though they showed little interest in cars.

- But, of course, all that was naive. Over the years, as he got deeper into the sport, first as an SCCA amateur and later as an FIA semi-pro, Larry noted clearly and often that racing could be, as the cliché goes, very hazardous to your health. There was a rich selection of ways, including sudden mortality, that one's anatomy could get messed up in a race car.

- Your ride might—or might not—be equipped with a proper roll bar. It could be strong enough to sustain a high-speed roll-over, or it could just be made of electrical conduit, which a man could bend with his bare hands. And it might be mounted so low that, even with you strapped in the seat, your head would jut above it, like a pumpkin on a fence post. Great-looking accessory ... as useless as spaghetti.

- You could be held in your seat by a web lap-belt—or you might prefer to go without one, your choice. With that little belt, if you should flip, your melon would hang out a foot or so beyond any roll bar, *thwupping* against the asphalt like a tether ball on a short rope. Without the belt, a violent incident such as a sideways crash with a competitor might send you flailing through the air like a two-year-old's rag doll.

- Fire ... never good ... was an ever-present threat, usually from loose fuel. But with cotton (and maybe some nylon) clothing and open helmets, there was really no discussion. It was imperative to avoid fire, and to get out quick should one happen.

- And happen it did. Safety fuel cells, at least for most cars, didn't exist yet. Traditional gas tanks were fabricated from metal and could be mounted front or back, inside the body work. Any impact (or even vibration) might puncture or split such tanks, releasing a gush of raw gas and fumes. Whether the accident was stopped or still moving, any spark, or just a hot exhaust system, would ignite the spreading cloud of highly volatile fuel.

- Hot! Flame so hot that a driver clothed in a one-layer cotton suit, freshly treated with boric acid compounds—solutions of Twenty Mule Team Borax for instance—had about five seconds before incurring second-degree burns. Third-degree burns followed quickly afterward. (By comparison, a modern two-layer Nomex suit, plus gloves, socks, shoes and balaclava, may provide a margin of forty to fifty seconds in a gasoline fire. Truly a lifesaving technology!)

- Course workers would approach immediately as they could, as near as they dared, and attempt to douse the fire with handheld CO2 or dry chemical extinguishers. The driver would be on his own until the flame could be quenched enough for corner workers to come in and help. However, corner workers' uniforms weren't generally treated with fire retardant, and they might or might not be wearing gloves. Their heads were bare or covered by caps. An unfortunate driver might be trapped or engulfed, in which case he was in very grim trouble—which is still the case today. In a bad one, he or she will melt down or burn up.

- The most common mishaps—collision and minor fire—occurred all the time, at nearly every race meeting, to all teams and skill levels. Drivers, mechanics, and pit crews were

human, soft and fragile and prone to errors. Race cars were elaborate gadgets, with lots of intricate functions and unyielding components and violent forces at work. They could break while moving at very fast speeds. Sometimes they injured one or more people in their vicinity.

- So, accidents happened, but they weren't inevitable. In thousands of miles of racing, driving a wide range of cars, including some high-performance ones, Larry had the good fortune not to be involved in a bad crash. He did have some close calls, came away with a few bruises and witnessed some real doozies.

- After dark: flood lighting in the early years was limited to the pits and front straight. Drivers depended on headlights and carefully aimed, high intensity driving lamps to navigate the mostly dark track. Imagine pools of focused light darting about, at high speed, through the night.

- At Daytona there was even an optical illusion to make things interesting. The soaring walls of the banking were lined along the top with warning lights for planes operating at the adjacent airport. When running the back straight, one's view far ahead—where the steeply tilted track should be—was a dark, towering shadow with a row of tiny "red stars" making an arc against the pitch-black sky.

- On one night lap in question, Larry more or less followed that arc and zipped down off the banking into the chute—to be met by a fireworks display.

- A moment earlier, just at the pit entrance, cars had collided in the middle of the track. Blinding headlights, still moving, flashed in all directions. Smoke and flame rose in flickering clouds. Larry could make out emergency vehicles approaching from behind the scenes and silhouettes of course workers running and readying extinguishers in the foreground.

- Larry was approaching this melee at 150 mph or so, with poor visibility and nowhere to go ... pit road blocked, hazards on left and walls on right and left, safety people (and who knew what else) straight ahead. He shut everything down ... *hard on the brakes, quick shifts down to first, a few sideways twitches from his rear-end* ... and managed to slow to a snail's pace. Workers waved him cautiously through the pileup, and he was off again to start the next lap. When he came around again, the mess was being cleaned up.

- The Ferrari had come through again. With its wide-open view, exceptional handling, superior brakes and gearbox, the GTO had made it possible to avoid turning a bad incident into an even uglier one.

- Later that night, walking through the pits, Larry encountered Jim Rathmann, his close neighbor in Melbourne Beach, Florida, and the 1960 Indy 500 winner. Jim just shook his head and shrugged. He'd seen lots of crashes.

· There is plenty of discourse about race drivers having a "death wish," as if they are haunted by some sinister suicidal tendency. They are not. They are simply willing to accept dares, to do things that may barely avert injury or death. But most race drivers are "cockeyed optimists," always looking on the bright side and almost never brooding about harm to themselves. They worry much more about accidentally injuring a course worker or a pit crew member or, worse, an innocent spectator.

· Even though conditions in those "good old days" could be deadly, Larry and others obviously took risks. Why did they engage in this reckless behavior? Because racing is not remotely like "going fast in a car." It involves a complex fusing of balance, dexterity, reflexes, visual acuity, sensation, skill, judgment, singular levels of competitiveness, daring and physical fitness, plus tons of practice to successfully drive fast. For most, the speeds, G-force and head-to-head competition are as addictive as drugs. Striking the balance—between risk and motivation—is a challenge undertaken by drivers in every race. The thrill of doing such an intricate, intoxicating thing transcends any thought of dying at it.

TV interviewer:
"So Larry, when did you start engaging in risk-taking?"
"Uh, I'm not sure … probably while I was being born."

Behind that flip answer there's a sincere thought. Perhaps for most males some level of risk-taking is built in. In Larry's day, most boys grew up climbing trees, jumping off barns, swinging over creeks on ropes, riding bicycles as fast as they could go, shooting at each other with BB guns and sling shots and Roman candles, shoving each other off logs, exploring caves and other forbidden places, soaring from high-dive boards, taking dares of every sort.

All this eventually morphed into organized sports and eventually into the workplace, where an acute competitive urge arose, focused on winning at all costs … life, limb and sometimes a limp. The truism, "a good loser is still a loser," was firmly embedded.

For some, a taste for thrills and a strong tolerance for uncertainty led to edgier activities, like extreme skiing, hang-gliding, rock-climbing, skydiving. And motor racing. Motor racing emerged when the second car was built, and now it's a fitting example of our innate human competitive drive.

"Risk-taking" also implies "risk-sharing," which might be reluctant or even resentful. Many drivers are married and have families. Those who don't usually have significant others. A few drivers forego these attachments as they feel it's irresponsible to form relationships that may abruptly end in tragedy. But all have someone who cherishes them and who would be thunderstruck to have them banged up.

For the most part, drivers' spouses, children, relatives, and lovers aren't involved in a decision to go racing. The sport is enticing though, and captures the imagination, so families and friends become part of a scene they enjoy immensely, or at least accommodate themselves to. So, it isn't useful to ask a driver's spouse, "How could you let them do this?" They don't have a vote. When the bug bites, the itch is relentless. But when a driver embarks to attend a race, it's impossible to know what the outcome may be. The odds are in favor of their safe return, but things can go wrong, and the results can be intense.

Finally, the competitive instinct deserves a mention. Every serious racer is driven by a voracious desire to win. Some, like A.J. Foyt (winner at Indy, Daytona, Le Mans and just about everywhere else), make no secret of it and bray about beating the competition at every opportunity. Others, like the late Lloyd Ruby (another winner with everything on four wheels), are unassuming and low key, but once behind the wheel they consistently go out and whip everybody's ass.

Even the great Grand Prix drivers, who tend to be a bit more self-effacing, will say that their motivation is going just fast enough to beat everybody else. Real competitors avoid talking and go all-out to win. As the great Stirling Moss said, "There are two things no man will admit that he cannot do well: drive and make love." With an attitude like that, is it any wonder that race drivers take some risks?

Chapter 23: **Carma**

"The wheel is come full circle."

—WILLIAM SHAKESPEARE

How could a man's destiny be so dramatically intertwined with that of a car? Did shared kismet bring them together or was it simply *chance?*

A famous-but-tragic entanglement was that of Ken Miles—a fellow competitor of Larry's—who engineered and raced the epochal Ford GT-40 to victory at Daytona and LeMans in 1966. It was a perfect blending, lap after lap, of man and machine. We can only imagine how tightly bonded Ken felt to his car; they were surely One. The larger full circle aspect is dramatized, although posthumously, many years later when Ken "raced again" as the protagonist of the major hit film *Ford vs. Ferrari.* The story, especially in its depiction onscreen, evokes romantic concepts of destiny and fate. And bigtime car racing.

Having been immersed in that era has left Larry wondering how it was that, during every single day in a decade of his life, his thoughts were dominated by racing. There was the race to the moon which defined his day job, and races in cars, which prevailed in his leisure hours, although there was little actual leisure, especially with The Car. And then how, one day, he walked away from it all, never to think about it obsessively again. And he wonders how, nearly half a century later, it returned to be a powerful force—one that rekindled his imagination, revved his competitive spirit, and restored a certain vitality.

Mastering the art of racing a Ferrari 250 GTO, surrounded by perils of 1960s tracks, was no doubt heady stuff. To compete nose to nose at top speed—to gain mere seconds of advantage, not knowing what the competition will do that may jeopardize one's lead,

203

or car, or life—must surely have been exhilarating. And winning? Nothing less than exultation.

But it is not the kind of experience that can come around again late in one's life, just as Tom Brady will not (probably!) win another Superbowl in his seventies. The thrills of 1960-1968 were reawakened for Larry, though not quite in the original way. However, what did occur was equally, if not more, sensational.

In the wheel of life, coming full circle provides the opportunity to step into a clearing of sorts. To see where we came from and where, at that moment, we are standing. This circular journey returning to Larry's past, his unlikely ride "back to the future," bestowed upon him a perspective he never dreamed. It became a thing of destiny, as it were—this opportunity to revisit one's youth, complete with his car, all the trappings and a cheering audience. And to work with an extraordinary team of people with a singular vision, as he had done during some of the best times of his life.

In being interviewed for this book, it was important for Larry to pause and examine the ground he had covered over that half-century. It allowed him to respect his courage, his trials, his achievements, and perseverance ... and of course his failings. Through reminiscence and writing, Larry came away with a deeper appreciation of who that young man was and how he had managed to not only survive and thrive but tackle the "unattainable" by never once considering anything as impossible.

As for the GTO, it doesn't think—rather, it's *thought about*. It arrived at a precise time when artistic design and flashy color and rash speed and take-no-prisoners-winning complemented each other. A time when Italian allure and Italian horsepower were on a roll. Car guys smoked, drank and bench-raced—hung out together, one-upping about their prowess in the cars. It was groovy to identify with racing champions, and so they did. Women desired to be involved and be noticed by them, and so they were. The Car got wrapped into this flaming hot package of personalities/tires/brakes/motors/smoke/metal that still sounds like rockets—and drivers that burned up the tracks and lived to tell about it.

Intrigued by speed, Larry searched the world in 1963 and found the ideal, once-in-a-lifetime race car; he sold it in 1966 after "driving the living shit out of it." He later found it, then lost it again for a long stretch. Then amazingly, in 2010, *it found him*. The GTO drove into Larry's radar once more and he was able to touch it, like a sort of magic talisman.

Before—during that long stretch—Larry and Petra had been driving ordinary cars, going like mad on one journey after another, working on space programs, racing here and there with abandon, freewheeling toward no hard destinations. Along the way, their ecstatic fun and adventure occasionally veered off (as happens to couples) into rough ruts of life and marriage. They got lost countless times, crashed into barriers, fell by waysides, were forced into detours, had breakdowns, ran out of gas, nearly succumbed to a DNF, but usually chose to "take the scenic route." All of which proves Petra's motto: *If you don't know where you're going, any road will take you there.*

Larry's motto may have been: *If you don't know where you're going, at least find a good car to take you there—fast.*

Just when destiny and fate seemed to have run their lifetime course, just when everything was a bit too ordinary, a little too predictable, winding down to the hum of a boring idle, was exactly when The Car reappeared to change everything up.

Larry and Sophia got to resume their passion where they'd left off, winning awards together again, becoming living legends ... and Petra—envisioning the story, its settings and all the remarkable players as a heartful, artful, over-the-moon romance—got to write about them and freeze the action forever. There's simply no better *carma* than that.

Now, like Shakespeare, they are "not of an age, but for all time."

Epilogue

A Letter to Wolfgang Graf Berghe von Trips

Dear Taffy,

This book has been a reflection on a story that began with you. Or rather, with your friendly gesture, introducing me to motor racing.

It was Saturday, December 3, 1960, during practice for the Nassau Trophy Race. We both thought it was an appealing idea to have a few casual laps around Oakes Field with Gordon Pennington's SWB berlinetta. You said, "Find a helmet, Larry, and join me. You'll understand it all better from the passenger seat."

After that riveting drive, and your astute running commentary—delivered calmly, as though we were simply enjoying a cup of coffee—I was dazzled by the whole experience. The rush of perceptions ... bursting out of corners, streaking down the straights, braking, sweeping through turns, overtaking, running close, the sense of control ... were not only new to me, but something I had apparently been wanting—needing?—all my life.

Back on the mainland, I was determined to go racing, and I did. I drove many events on many circuits in an assortment of cars. But my eye was always on the big contenders in the big cars. When I finally got my chance, in my own Ferrari 250 GTO, with a top crew and high-level competition, I was in my element, in the kind of endeavor that you taught me to appreciate.

At Nassau neither of us could have imagined that you would lose your life a few months later. We couldn't know that I would create a bronze sculpture of you, or be reminiscing about this now, after nearly sixty years. But wherever you are, I thank you for helping me find extraordinary direction and accomplishment.

Sincerely,

Larry

A Letter to Wayne Obry

Dear Wayne,

I haven't had many encounters with geniuses. And fewer still with gifted people who became good friends. In your case, I'm humbled to have had both.

You were a dream-weaver and a master synthesizer. People brought their wispy uncertain fantasies to you, and with your magic flair you turned them into priceless reality. You would tell us you were a "Wisconsin country boy," but you were internationally renowned for your historical acumen, technical intensity, and the power of the team you led. You could even (sometimes) practice patience with idiots. You were a family man, a car guy and a partner with airtight integrity. We crossed paths with each other late, but in seconds we became close.

You brought our story full circle in a way that no one else could possibly have done. I only wish that you could be here to read what Petra and I have captured in print and continue to carry in our hearts.

Love,

Larry

Sadly, Wayne Obry passed away on March 11, 2016. It was an unexpected and tragic loss for his wife, Debbie, their family, their many friends, the staff of MPI and the entire global community of Ferrari aficionados. Wayne was truly a remarkable, accomplished, unpretentious man who will be missed for a long time.

Full Circle

And you're back!
   at the front
      on top of your game
        zooming over
      the finish
to start once again

First, a pause …
   look around
      the places you've been
        behold all that was
      many wins
and great friends

What a journey
   it's made you
      the man you are now
        ever better
      each lap
so please take a bow

ꝏ

~ Petra Perkins

Glossary of Racing Lingo

Agricultural racing
Scornful slang for accidentally running off the track and roaming among weeds, trees and shrubbery. (In the '60s, most courses were devoid of safety barriers and were lined with hay bales, peach baskets, rubber cones, grazing cattle and clueless spectators.)

Aero
Short for aerodynamics; anything to do with a car's air flow efficiency; see "down-force"

Alloy
Lightweight, rigid car wheel, cast from nonferrous metal alloy

Apex
Innermost spot on a corner, after which the turn opens out onto the following straight. In a sense, the apex is the point of the whole thing.

Aquaplane
Skid on a sheet of water; tires lose adhesion and driver becomes a passenger; may result in agricultural racing

Back-marker
Slow car, trailing the pack, not in contention; see "moving chicane"

Berzerka
Wild, frantic confusion and fury; *"The pit stop turned into a berzerka, with guys grabbing the wrong tools and spilling stuff and tripping over one another."*

Binders
Slang for "brakes"

Brain fade
Failure to concentrate while approaching a corner at speed; often leads to spin-outs, agricultural racing and/or crashes

Brake fade
Dangerous condition afflicting a car's brakes while approaching a corner at speed; may be a persistent, deteriorating problem; often leads to spinouts, agricultural racing, and/or crashes

Car guy
Human being, any gender, suffering a disorder relating to all things automotive; not quite as seriously infected as a gearhead

Chicane
Series of esses or linked zig-zag corners; see "moving chicane"

Clod
Slang for a very bad, slow, maybe decrepit race car; also "dog," "pig," "slug," "shit-box" Or, in dirt track racing, a lump of clay thrown by a spinning tire

Clod guard
Dirt track racing term: fiberglass shield to stop clods hitting drivers with massive force, maybe breaking ribs or smearing one's make-up

Corner
n. A turn or bend connecting two straights on a racing circuit
v. Execute a turn; to be engaged in "cornering"

Crash
Catch-all term: 5 mph bump on the grid; 100 mph car-to-car wallop on-track; ass-over-tea-kettle-roll-'er-up-in-a-ball; everything in between. Stock car folks say "wreck;" Brits prefer "shunt;" (It's all the same … a hot mess)

Crash hat
Slang for "helmet," "brain bucket," "skid lid"

Deep (go deep)
To delay braking, going as far into a corner as feasible, getting competitive advantage. Has no intellectual or sexual inference

Dog box (also crash box)
Rugged reliable transmission with spur-cut gears and no synchronizers; usually shifted by double-clutching; sounds at all times like it will soon disintegrate; it won't

Double-clutch
Using clutch pedal twice to down-shift. Matches engine and gearbox speeds for smoother shifting, less wear and tear. *Off the gas, clutch in, shift to neutral, clutch out, quick tap on gas, clutch in, shift into lower gear, clutch out, back on gas*: see "heel-and-toe"

Downforce
Aerodynamic reverse lift; permits faster speeds through corners by increasing vertical force on the tires, creating more grip; provided by aerodynamic body shapes, wings and deflectors; not a "free lunch" as more downforce produces more drag, slowing the car. Different from *G-force*

Downshift
Engage transmission in lower gear for more low-speed torque. Driver's Commandment: "Thou shalt never, ever slow your car by downshifting." It's hard on engines, clutches and those cute little toothy things

in your gearbox. Helpful mnemonic: *"Gears are for going; brakes are for slowing."*

DNF, DNS, DQ
Race results: "Did Not Finish;" "Did Not Start;" "Disqualified"

Drive
Racing job; *"I got a drive in the #42 Porsche next season. It's slower than a dead stump, but it beats sitting on the pit wall."*

Dry sump
Engine design using a shallow sump, big external reservoir, oil cooler, multiple pumps. Advantages = low engine profile, high reliability, reduced oil surging, better cooling. Disadvantages = heavy, many moving parts; lots of people don't know what you're talking about

FIA
Federation Internationale de l'Automobile; governing body for professional racing world-wide; see "SCCA"

Flag
Universal race signalling method. Trackside officials show flags to passing drivers, in lieu of other communications. Colors indicate flags' meaning and are instantly recognizable. Ignoring a flag is a serious infraction.

Green flag: *The Start*; *everybody GO ... NOW*

Red flag: *Emergency; everybody STOP ... NOW*

Yellow flag: *Caution; approaching a problem area; DO NOT PASS*

Waving yellow flag: *No kidding; watch out; be prepared to stop*

Yellow flag with red stripes: *Oil on the track; don't try any heroic moves*

Black flag: *You've been very naughty; report to the pit stewards ASAP*

Black flag with orange "meat ball": *Your car seems to be coming apart; go to pits*

Blue flag: *Give way; you're blocking a faster car*

Waving blue flag: *How many times must I tell you?*

White flag: *Emergency vehicle on circuit; may be anywhere, going in any direction*

Checkered flag: *It's over; let's have a beer*

Gatorade
First-ever sports drink developed at University of Florida with small contribution by Team BARF lab rats. Rats ... er ... drivers drank cloudy electrolyte solution, spiked with lemon extract, before stints in the car. They experienced improved hydration, reduced fatigue in brutally hot conditions. Stuff had unforgettable chemical taste. It is now a delicious brightly-hued thirst quencher. To this day, though, Larry does not particularly enjoy Gatorade, no matter what color.

Gearhead
Person (nearly always male) intensely and perpetually immersed in all things automotive and mechanical; much more severely afflicted than simple "car guy"

G-force (in multiples of gravity)
Inertial force imposed on all three axes of race cars and drivers when accelerating, braking, cornering and going over bumps and dips; on long sweeping corners it's known as a "neck stretcher." G-force is especially notable on high-speed banked turns. It is variable and may range between 2-G and 5-G. (Gibbons also experience this effect while swinging through trees, so is it really "Gibbon-force?") see *downforce*

Go pedal
Accelerator, throttle, gas

Grid
Assembly of cars in orderly pattern on track for start of a race. May be standing start or rolling start; see "Le Mans start"

Groupie
Usually young, attractive, female fan enthralled with one or more race drivers; often prone to unambiguous acts of admiration and submission; has little regard for cars, racing, or drivers' wives or girlfriends; see "pit bunny"

Heel-and-toe
Technique used in double-clutching; allows smooth, rapid downshifts while slowing for corners. *Right foot presses both brake and accelerator, usually the toe does the braking while heel bumps the gas pedal. Double-clutch maneuver is done simultaneously with left foot. Protects hardware by matching engine and gearbox revs while keeping continuous pressure on the brakes.* Technique may be required multiple times, downshifting from, say, fifth gear to second going into a slow corner; takes plenty of practice, is slightly different for every car. Failure to heel-and-toe is a fine way to quickly trash a perfectly good transmission and clutch; see "double-clutch"

Hot shoe
Fast driver; see "lead foot"

Hurry
Slang for driving fast and/or aggressively

Inside line
Approach to corner nearest apex side; slowest line but may best permit overtaking especially when traffic obstructs outside lines

Knockoff
Type of wheel, secured with a single threaded hub tightened and loosened with a massive lead "knockoff hammer." *Tidbit*: knockoffs have right-handed threads on

car's left side and left-handed threads on the other to prevent self-loosening under heavy acceleration (think about it)

Lead foot ("led")
Fast driver; one with a heavy right foot, ostensibly made of lead; see "hot shoe"

Le Mans start
Standing start used for many years, notably at Sebring and Le Mans. Cars were stationed along pit wall on one side of track, drivers on the other. When flag dropped, drivers sprinted across, got into their cars, started up, drove away. Sometimes they ran to the wrong cars. Roadster drivers often avoided doors, running up hoods and leaping over windscreens into seats. Sometimes cars wouldn't start. In the era before five-point harnesses, drivers often ignored seat belts. The practice was abandoned in 1970 as being dangerous, pointless, and stupid.

Lift
Lift one's foot; lessen pressure on the gas; slow down; see "shutoff"

Line
Path taken through a corner; ideal line is smooth arc with longest-possible radius, starting on outside verge, clipping inside apex and opening up to follow outside verge; under nominal conditions all other lines will be slower. In theory, a single lap describes one continuous perfect line

around the circuit adjusted for corner and traffic conditions

Marbles
Sticky little clumps of tire rubber collecting off-line at corners; they affect adhesion and drivers avoid them; may also include pea gravel. With open-faced helmets and small windscreens of yore, this stuff, thrown up by cars ahead, stung like hell one's nose, lips and cheeks

Marker
See "shutoff point"

Marque
Fancy word for brand or make; used mostly by car snobs and snobby car writers

Moving chicane
Slang for a driver following a wobbly irregular line, making himself hard to pass

Nomex
Flame-resistant fabric; modern drivers' multi-layer clothing—suits, long underwear, balaclavas, socks, gloves, helmet lining and shoes—are made of and/or lined with Nomex; prevents third-degree burns for many seconds in intense fire, affording drivers time to exit and safety workers to suppress fire. (Nomex came into use, mostly by USAC, in 1966; Larry Perkins wore an early J. B. Hinchman suit with clod-guard pockets on the chest.)

OA
Race finishing position; "position Overall"

Outside line
Racing line on outer edge of a corner; slower than ideal but often necessary in traffic

Over-steer
Tendency for car to lose adhesion at rear, or "swap ends," in a corner; controlled with corrective steering and application of power; terminal over-steer results in a spin; see "sideways," "under-steer," "agricultural racing"

Pit bunny
Specimen of young female wildlife frequently found prowling the pits in search of certain forms of prey and nourishment; see "Groupie"

Plow
Car's tendency to go straight ahead in a corner; see "push," "under-steer"

Push
See "plow," "under-steer"

Redline
RPM limit; indicated by red mark or needle on tachometer dial; Driver's Commandment: *"Thou shalt never, ever rev past the redline"* Punishment for breaking commandment: severe shunning by chief mechanic and pit crew

Revs
n. Engine speed, revolutions-per-minute; see "RPM"
v. Accelerate engine in neutral; *"He just revs it to hear the sweet music."*

Ride
Race driver's job; *"I got a ride in the Ferrari GTO for next season;"* see "drive," "seat"

Roundel
Large white circle on sides, front and rear of a race car; provides prominent background for race numbers. Sometimes crews screw up, putting different numbers on different roundels, "41" on one side, "14" on the other; officials are not amused.

RPM
Engine speed in revolutions per minute; also rpm; see "revs"

Rubber
Slang for "tires;" rubber on Brit cars is spelled "tyres"

SCCA
Sports Car Club of America: automobile club and sanctioning body supporting road racing, rallying, autocross, other speed events. Formed in 1944, runs programs for amateur and professional racers; coordinates with FIA in staging international events in the U.S.

Seat
Race driver's job; see "drive," "ride"

Shit-box
Rude slang for any sloppy-looking, badly performing, possibly dangerous car. *"I don't need a ride in that shit-box."* See also "slug" and "clod."

Shooting brake
Brit for station wagon, as in, *"Toss the spanners, snap-jack and spare bits in the shooting brake and we'll carry on."*

Shutoff point
Spot approaching a corner where driver lifts off gas and starts braking, with smallest possible delay in between; it's difficult using depth perception alone. During practice drivers pick visual cues along trackside as aids in this; different lines need different shutoffs; it's stupid to pick a marker that may move, like, say, a course worker; missing a marker may result in agricultural racing; see "heel-and-toe," "lift," "marker."

Sideways
Undesirable car attitude in a corner; sometimes caused by "overcooking," as in *"He overcooked it going into Turn 4 and ended up sideways in crazy traffic."* See "over-steer."

Skid lid
Slang for "helmet;" see "crash hat"

Slam the door
Sudden maneuver by competitor to impede an attempt to overtake

Slug
Slang for very low-performance car; *"I got last place in that slug with no effort at all."*

Speedo
Short for "speedometer;" dashboard instrument giving woefully inaccurate display of how fast, or slow, a car is going. Many race cars have no speedo as no one cares; the point is to go as fast as possible at all times.

Spoiler
Rear-end airfoil or wing providing aero enhancement of grip; see "down-force"

Spy
See "tell-tale"

Stagger
1. Tire setup, with uneven pressure side-to-side; adjusts performance on certain tracks
2. Gait of a winning driver after groping and French-kissing the race queen and guzzling all the champagne in sight

Strap on (a car)
Slang for "get in and go"

Spy
See tell-tale

Tach (pron. "tack")
Short for "tachometer," dashboard instrument displaying engine speed in RPM

Tell-tale
Friction-mounted needle on tach, used to set redline and detect over-revving by drivers; reset knob is purposely concealed from drivers as they cannot be trusted; see "redline," "spy"

Under-steer
Tendency of car to lose adhesion at the front and continue straight ahead in a corner; usually due to imbalance in weight distribution and/or terrible tires; see "agri-cultural racing," "plow," "push"

Wing
Aerodynamic structure on car; designed to enhance down-force and grip

Wire wheel
Race car wheel with wire spokes; commonly used during 1960s and earlier; advantage was light weight; disadvantage; finicky and fragile; supplanted by alloys. See "knock-off."

Works
n. European/British term for "factory"
v. Driver's complaint: *Sometimes the brake pedal works; sometimes it goes to the floor.*

Wrench
n. Term for common hand-tool; also, slang for "mechanic"
v. To act as a dedicated mechanic; *"He wrenched on my Ferrari a year. It was never the same afterward."*

Photo Credits

Bibliography

Baime, A.J., *Go Like Hell*, 2010, New York, NY, Houghton Mifflin Harcourt

Bluemel, Keith, *Ferrari GTO 250,* 1998, Bay View Books

Boe, Alan, *Cavallino Magazine*, 2012, Cavallino Inc.

Cannell, Michael, *The Limit,* 2011, Atlantic Books

Daley, Robert, *The Cruel Sport,* 1963, Prentice-Hall International

Hinton, Ed, *Daytona*, 2001, New York, NY, Warner Books

Galanos, Louis and Petra Perkins, *SportsCarDigest.com; "*A Good Car (*Guy*) Is Hard to Find: A Girl's Memoir," Feb. 1, 2019, *Sports Car Digest*

Hinton, Ed, *Daytona*, 2001, New York, NY, Warner Books

Karr, Mary*, The Art of Memoir,* 2005, Harper Collins

MacGregor, Jeff, *Sunday Money,* 2005, Harper-Collins

McCluggage, Denise, *By Brooks Too Broad for Leaping,* 1994, Fulcorte Press

Noctoras, Kelly, *The Book You Were Born to Write*, 2018, Hay House

Perkins, Larry, *Velocetoday.com,* "The GTO and the Hole in the Donut," Oct. 29, 2019, Peter Vack

Taruffi, Piero and Juan Manuel Fangio, *The Technique of Motor Racing*, 1990, Robert Bentley

Williams, David, *Prancing Horse Magazine,* Ferrari Club of America

Yates, Brock, *Enzo Ferrari: The Man and the Machine,* 1991, DoubleDay

Acknowledgments

We extend our heartfelt gratitude and appreciation to the following people and organizations who have given us support, encouragement (large and small), or in some way participated in the development of this project over several years. Hereby, please be recognized! Many thanks for your time and interest. ~ Larry & Petra

• Bill Eve • Paul Gilpatrick • Jeff Allison • John Siscoe • David Seielstad • David Gizzi • Alan Boe • Ferrari Club of America (Rocky Mountain) • Scuderia di Bari • Bert Smith • Mick Victor • Denver Woman's Press Club • Louis Galanos • Faulkner Society • Michael Smith • Jeff Kleinman • Janie Tippins • Sam Southworth • Bob Rodamer • Dr. Bob Bodin • Peter Vack • John & Steve Mastroianni • Wally Hampton • Wendy Hampton • Tom Morgan • Debbie Obry • Mario Andretti • Motion Products Inc • John Barnes • Carl Nelson & Denise Larsen • Nick Mason • Michael Fisher • Tim Nevinson (Veloce Press) • Michael Standlee • Tom Ulrich • Janet Wilson • Jeanne & Trooper Thornton • Spike Snyder • Becki & Larry Perkins Jr. • Marcel Massini • Marcel DeLorean • Michele Sires-DeLorean • Gail Waldstein • Connie Boyle • Andrew Herrala • Brooke Granville • John & Kirby Palm • Jim & Nancy Stainton • Jim Rowe • Bill Patterson • Karen DeGroot Carter • Jackie Sachen Turner • Chuck Turner • Kim Smith • Mike Surline • John Surline • Shawn Surline • Faye Dixon • Sue McDonald • Liz Maddux • Dr. Jim Maddux • Darla Rae–Women in Film & Media of Colorado •
Lighthouse Writers: Emily Rapp Black, Prof. Robin Hemley, Shari Caudron, Steve Almond, Andre Dubus III, Jannette Matusiak, Gene Marsh, Sheila McAuliffe, Lia Woodall, Ellen Nordberg, Jacqueline St. Joan, Nancy Sharp

• ... And last (never last in racing) but the best... cherished friend Denise McCluggage who provided inspiration and her enthusiastic Foreword in the early stage of our book (2012-14).

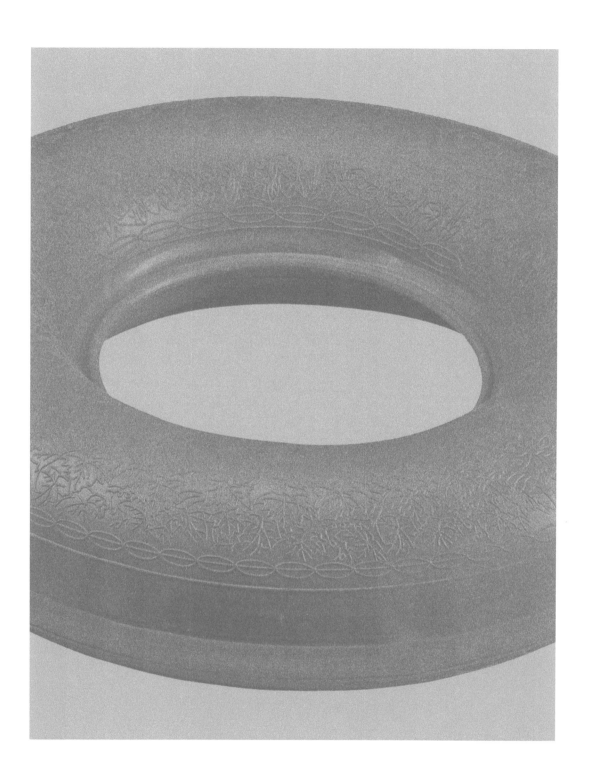

A Bonus Story: The GTO and the Hole in the Donut

Sebring, Florida, March 1964.
We were off to the races.
And I had piles.

For a few select days each spring, a caravan of car haulers and racing fans weaves its way into the tranquil little orange-grove town on "The Ridge"—the lake-dotted high-ground running along the spine of the Sunshine State.

One might think, "What an unlikely spot for a big motorsport event." But by the mid-60s Sebring had made its place in the lists for over a decade and would again be hosting the "12-Hour Grand Prix of Endurance."

I had visited here twice before—in 1959 for the first U.S. Grand Prix and, improbably, the following year as a guest of the Bill Sturgis team, with Gordon Pennington's Ferrari 250 GT SWB. This time I would be driving my Ferrari 250 GTO, with what we hoped was a chance to win something in this infamously difficult road race.

But now there was a disturbing development—I had horrific hemorrhoids.

A case of the piles is a diabolical thing. We all know about the Seven Deadly Sins, but if there are also Ten Terrible Torments, this bottom-dwelling monster tops the list.

"Whom the piles grips is transformed in one instant from man to shark; and like the shark that must remain in perpetual motion, so the sufferer of piles writhes and twists, bending and quaking in ceaseless turmoil. From between his teeth come sounds so primitive as to make the skin creep. He would sell his birthright, forfeit his honor or his

*name, even kill to rid himself of agony. And like a maddened beast, he lashes out at all
who come near."*

~ paraphrasing Dr. Richard Selzer

This malady produces itching discomfort that morphs into nearly intolerable hot pain
in a very inconvenient corner of one's anatomy. It hurts—and bleeds—whether one stands,
kneels, or lies down. And it really throbs when you sit. It is hugely aggravated when you sit
on something bouncy and jolting—like the seat of a race car. And nowhere could a race car
bounce or jolt more than on that primitive old circuit at Sebring.

In 1964, arrival for an endurance race pretty much followed a standard procedure. The
crew unloaded the prepared car from the trailer and moved it to the garage ... if they were
so lucky as to have one. The road grime was cleaned up and the whole rig got a quick once-
over, which included running the engine to ensure that it would pass official scrutineering
(technical inspection).

Routine paperwork was sorted out, and the car was driven to the inspection site in
Sebring's central circle—a picturesque park at the hub of the tiny business sector, five
miles from the track. There experts examined, measured, weighed and certified it for rules
compliance, mechanical readiness and safety. The inspectors applied a non-removable
sticker where it could be easily seen by pit stewards, and the car was released to enter the
track. In those days, the drivers' outfits also got a perfunctory check; the clothing was cotton, and some of the helmets were basically modified polo headgear. Safety, for the most
part, was an afterthought.

If there was a glitch, if the car failed tech, then the crew had to deal with the disruption.
Sometimes the violation was minor—a loose part or wire, say—but it could be more serious, like a fluid leak, or a bad driving lamp, or some part of the bodywork out of spec. Then
the team had to really get busy because all-important practice sessions would be starting
promptly. After corrections, the car needed to go all the way back to scrutineering for final
approval. And, as with everything in motor racing, time was critical.

The team drivers were not idle during all of this preparation. After all, it was our
butts in the seat, and we had a vital interest in tuning up this complicated collection of
tools called "the car." We were active members of the crew, and one with a bad case of

hemorrhoids was not a big help. It was torture, but practice loomed, and I tried hard to hold up my end.

"Practice?" you might say. "If you've run here before, and the car's ready, who needs practice?" The answer is that every trip to every track is different. The car has been freshly prepared, often with a rebuilt motor, so it contains a whole shopping list of unknowns. The track surface has changed since your last visit—will inevitably change some more during practice. The crew needs to reaccustom themselves with the pit facilities. The drivers need track time to get into the groove. The stewards need to familiarize themselves with the cars and teams. Qualifying for starting positions is run during practice.

Finally, an endurance race is just that—your car must withstand quite a few laps of practice, ensuring its ability to endure twelve hours of unrelenting hammering that will stress every nut, bolt and washer to the max in head-to-head competition. Drivers' fitness is key too, enabling them to endure and excel. To simply finish the Sebring race, whatever your final position, has long been considered a certain mark of success.

By Friday, my unwelcome affliction had not improved. The practice sessions had tormented it pretty intensely, and I now began to imagine evil spirits … demons that were somehow angered and visiting their excruciating vengeance on me. They formed a cluster of pulsating fireballs lurking you-know-where. The race would begin at ten the next morning. There was no way I could start like this. I desperately needed to do something.

Then I ran into a local guy in the pit lane: "Larry, that's murder … you gotta see Doc. He'll have something." Doc wasn't a physician; his real name was Phil, and he was a pharmacist who presided over Sebring's only drugstore. In our special world of busted knuckles and frequent burns and stuff too nasty to breathe, a sort of medical fix-it guy was more indispensable than a regular doctor. Everyone relied on Doc for advice and over-the-counter snake oil that racing people always need.

I headed downtown and found the drugstore in a charming old brick storefront on the circle. Inside, with his starched white coat, rimless glasses, and easy smile, Doc conveyed compassion, authority, reassurance. Unfortunately, though, he advised there wasn't much he or anybody else could do.

The standard treatments were applications of an ointment called Preparation H that had been around for thirty years and sitz baths with Epsom salts that have been around for centuries.

Doc provided me with a squeeze-tube of Preparation H and a big sack of salts. But then he had a brainstorm. "What you need is something to sit on, to insulate your nether region from the battering that track is sure to deliver. I have just the thing." He rummaged under the counter and produced a little inflatable red rubber donut. "It's used, so I can't sell it," Doc said, "but I'll lend it and you can return it after you win that race."

Encouraged, I took Doc's nostrums and his rubber lifesaver and rushed to my hotel room to start the cure. Lying in a tub, I applied Doc's magic, steeping one end of me in hot Epsom brine and chilling the other with a couple of icy vodka gimlets. I had to skip the

last-minute work with the crew, but next morning, after applying gobs of Preparation H, I was able to stand, walk, and (most importantly) sit without groaning in anguish.

So, here's the picture: During the running of the 1964 Sebring 12 Hours, we had to manage my damn donut along with every-thing else. Drop it in the seat at pit stops before I jumped in; retrieve it when I turned over to Bill; make sure it stayed inflated and nothing punctured it; keep oil and fuel off it. And the thing was just thick enough to make squeezing into the car twice as challenging when I was in a helluva hurry.

Did it work? Well, it wasn't a silver bullet, but once in place it made life in the cockpit tolerable for several hours at a time. We had a competitive car, a great crew and a super-fast co-driver, Bill Eve. There was plenty of extra excitement, with a huge crash and fire quite near us on the pit straight. It's hard to worry about your bottom line when you're busy trying to get on top of all those things.

And, in fact, we did win something. We endured mechanical trouble and a couple of long pit stops, dropping us down the list of finishers. But so did other teams. We managed to take third in Class GT 12, for which we received a small check, a nice Heuer stopwatch and a silver cup that I still treasure (but often forget to polish). Like I said, finishing Sebring is a feather in one's cap … and possibly a trophy on one's shelf.

When I returned Phil's donut, I assured him we had taken good care of it. And I told him, "Doc, that thing really saved my ass."

Doc smiled and nodded wisely—as shamans and medicine men are inclined to do.

Author Bios

Larry Perkins quit driving in 1969 to further his aerospace career. Following retirement, he began sculpting, and created an award-winning bronze action figure of World Champion Phil Hill. Larry's long-ago campaign with the Ferrari GTO is captured in this extraordinary memoir.

Petra Perkins, a storyteller from childhood, retired from aerospace engineering and became a widely-published author. She has won the Faulkner-Wisdom Gold Medal in Poetry and was nominated for the Pushcart Prize in creative non-fiction. (www.petrapetra.com). Petra, at 15, witnessed Larry's car at a race in Sebring, Florida, but did not know a Ford from a Ferrari. Or that GTOs were famous, until she met the driver when she was 30. She "met" The Car 30 years after that, and finally understood everything.

Printed in the USA
CPSIA information can be obtained
at www.ICGtesting.com
LVHW060836180124
769213LV00004B/66